Piecing Together the Past

Piecing Together the Past

The Interpretation of Archaeological Data

V. Gordon Childe

AAKAR

Piecing Together the Past
V. Gordon Childe

First Aakar Edition 2018

ISBN 978-93-5002-543-7

Published by
AAKAR BOOKS
28 E Pocket IV, Mayur Vihar Phase I
Delhi 110 091, India
aakarbooks@gmail.com
www.aakarbooks.com

Printed at
D.K. Fine Art Press, Delhi 110 052

Preface

ARCHÆOLOGICAL technique has been expounded lucidly and even vividly in several recent manuals. Atkinson, Cookson and Kenyon, Crawford and Wheeler have admirably explained how archæologists can identify, recover, record and conserve data for history. The methods and theories used in classifying such data and in extracting history from them have not been so comprehensively and systematically explained in any modern English book. Yet to interpret and even to recognize their proper data archæologists are forced to make certain peculiar assumptions though these be seldom formulated explicitly; they have elaborated distinctive categories for their classification; they in fact employ—not always consistently—a whole assemblage of common words in highly uncommon specialized senses. Since 1946 I have been accustomed every alternate year to devote a course of lectures to the principles of archæological classification, the current terminology and the implicit interpretative concepts. The present book is based upon these lectures.

Its aim is to explain the words to which professional archæologists, like myself, do give technical meanings, the methodological hypotheses we invoke and the postulates underlying our procedures. The exposition cannot avoid being critical; inconsistencies of nomenclature and practice are too glaring and too confusing to be ignored. I have ventured to suggest a few emendations, but I have no intention of adopting them myself and no expectation that my colleagues will. So I have refrained from proposing any ideally logical system of classification and terminology. Once the reader understands what current terms really mean, he will recognize how confusing and ambiguous they may be and should be able to discount consequential errors.

I have taken my examples almost entirely from prehistoric archæology, archæology unaided by texts, because the most distinctively archæological concepts and methods were devised just for this branch. But these concepts and methods can be applied—and profitably applied—to all branches of archæology. Those of my colleagues who deal with inscribed documents and with data described in written texts, can often short-circuit the laborious procedures alone available to the prehistorian. Still, till the sixteenth century the history of applied science has to be based almost exclusively on archæological data, and for the recognition and classification of processes and implements, such as screws and braces, the prehistorians' techniques must often be invoked. If Romanists and medievalists could be persuaded to adopt the techniques and the categories elaborated for older periods, many problems in history might be resolved. Archæology is one. The concepts discussed here are applicable to all its branches.

V. GORDON CHILDE

March 1955

Contents

CHAPTER ONE

What is Archæology About?

ARCHÆOLOGY studies all changes in the material world that are due to human action—naturally in so far as they survive. The archæological record is constituted of the fossilized results of human behaviour, and it is the archæologist's business to reconstitute that behaviour as far as he can and so to recapture the thoughts that behaviour expressed. In so far as he can do that, he becomes an historian. The aim of this book is therefore to explain how archæologists order their data to form a record and how they may try to interpret them as concrete embodiments of thoughts.

The most familiar surviving results of behaviour are of course the things men have made or unmade which may be called artifacts. These include on the one hand tools, weapons, personal ornaments, charms, statuettes, and on the other farm-houses, temples, castles, canals, mineshafts, graves. It is convenient to divide artifacts into two classes—relics and monuments. The former are portable and can be removed to a museum or laboratory for study. Monuments are either earth-fast or too massive to remove and have to be studied on the spot.

But not all archæological data belong to one or other of these classes, nor can be called artifacts at all. A Mediterranean shell found in a reindeer hunter's cave in Central France is not an artifact, not having itself been altered by man. But its presence in Central France several hundred miles from its nearest natural habitat is a result of human action and as such an archæological datum; for shells do not fly and no known natural agency would carry the cowrie shell from the Gulf of Lions to the valley of the Vezère that flows into the Bay of Biscay. So its transport is a very significant archæological phenomenon.

Again the interment of a body, crouched on its left side facing south, is the result of human action, but cannot be called an artifact. One house in the Late Bronze Age village of Buchau was twice as big as all the rest and more elaborate in construction. Such relations between monuments or relics are very significant archæological phenomena from which historical inferences can be drawn, but are themselves neither monuments nor relics. The relations of monuments and relics to the non-human environment too may be archæological data. The location of settlements in relation to good fishing grounds, to easily cultivable soil or to sheltered harbours may give a decisive clue as to the activities and economy of the settlers. The natural environment is at once an incentive and a limit to human action. At the same time man's intervention may itself profoundly affect the environment, exterminating some animals and introducing others, clearing forests and turning grassy steppes into dust-bowls. These changes are strictly the result of human action, but cannot usually be defined by normal archæological techniques, but only with the aid of methods devised by the natural sciences—botany, zoology, climatology and geology. And their aid must be invoked too in determining the unmodified environment which, quite apart from human intervention, has undergone vast changes during the period of man's existence on the earth. The importance for archæology of these phenomena that must be studied by other disciplines has been recognized in the University of London by the creation of a Department of Environmental Archæology—a precedent followed by other universities in Britain and on the Continent.

Nor should the purview of the archæologist be more limited in time. The loose nut that dropped off my car on Haverstock Hill this morning, the sardine tin I neatly buried after lunch on Esher Common and the crater left by a misdirected German bomb are archæological data just as much as the laurel leaf blade broken and thrown away by a Solutrean reindeer hunter, the Floddan Wall round Edinburgh or the Ramasseum at Karnak. Much of the archæologist's material is horribly like the first three examples. If we do not study such things yet, it is because we have more complete sources of information in eyewitnesses' reports or printed accounts. In the light of these not all the events I mention would seem worthy of inclusion in serious history. But when a rain of hydrogen bombs have destroyed the written records of Europe and North America, a Fuegian archæologist in 5555 may be reduced to precisely this sort of junk in reconstructing the history of what is now called England. Of course he will not be able to identify Professor Childe as the driver of the car whose nut became embedded in the roadway of Haverstock Hill nor as the burier of a sardine tin on Esher Common.

In fact archæologists as such deal, and must deal, only with abstractions, what we call *types*. We may admit as a 'type', not just 'nuts', but only 'hexagonal $\frac{5}{8}$ in. . . . nuts'. But for us all nuts answering to this specification are the same, are instances of the type. Archæologists as such are not the least interested in differences between individual nuts of the specified type—nor is the reader. By themselves the scraps just mentioned would mean no more to a student in the sixth millennium than to one of the second. In conjunction with other scraps of the same order they may acquire significance. With no better techniques than my contemporaries possess, the archæologist of the sixth millennium could read these scraps as documents illustrative of the sort of vehicle used on roads round a vast city, the tidy habits of some of its citizens and the objectives of nameless enemies.

These are the sort of things in which archæologists, like historians—nay, as historians—are interested—human actions and thoughts. It is only because they are results of human behaviour, and therefore express human thinking, that archæologists eagerly collect, scrupulously measure and record and systematically classify bits of junk and holes in the ground. This at once distinguishes archæology from philately, the collection of relics from the collection of snuff-boxes. Collectors of stamps or snuff-boxes may be just as keen in accumulating items, just as minute in their description and just as scientific in their classification. But the contents of their collections are valued primarily for themselves; their worth is determined by their intrinsic qualities, primarily scarcity. The archæologist's quarry is valued only as a clue to something else—the activity and mentality of their makers and users.

In much the same way the archæologist's approach might be contrasted to that of the connoisseur and art-historian. The latter's objects are of course archæological data, being expressions of human thought. But they are judged primarily by their intrinsic beauty. Secondly a work of art—painting, statue or building—just because it is of value in itself, is prized irrespective of the context in which it is found. Indeed we tear down the frieze from a temple in a sunny clime and set it at eye-level in a room in murky London to appreciate its beauty! On the other hand the value of an archæological object, the extent to which it can answer historical questions, depends mainly on its context. An isolated nut is not a thing of beauty and hardly a rarity. Only because it was found embedded in a particular layer of tarmac and because similar nuts of the same type are to be found in still more significant contexts—even holding together bits of cars—can it reveal human purposes. Few archæological documents are in themselves beautiful or even informative. But most belong to types instances of which have been found in contexts—with, or in, or containing, other objects—which give a clue as to their function, to their meaning to their makers and users.

Finally an object of art is individual and unique; archæological data are abstract types. Of course any product of man's handiwork is really unique. Obviously no two Gothic churches or Norman castles are identical and a little closer inspection would reveal comparable though less conspicuous differences between two horseshoes forged in Little Puddleton in 1863 or two tanged-and-barbed arrow-heads from the Beaker layer at Maiden Castle. Still, the individual members of each of these four pairs exhibit certain common features, repeated in both of them and indeed in all members of the class that is the denotation of the common designation. Archæologists consider phenomena almost exclusively as members of a class or, as they say, instances of a type. They ignore that it is the particular peculiarities, accidental or intentional, that in fact distinguish each specimen.

Archæologists, it is true, go on refining distinctions and sharpening discrimination so that things once lumped together as a group representing a single type are broken up between a growing number of types. As the number of types discriminated grows, each becomes more concrete, defined by more and more distinctive characters. But an archæological datum as such must remain an abstraction, an instance of a type. It can never attain the full concreteness of individuality and remain an object for archæological study. A really unique creation, the result of an act never repeated nor imitated, would slip through the archæologist's classificatory net and thus elude his interpretation unless it were helped out by some extraneous circumstance—a contemporary written description or an explanatory inscription. It might become an *objet d'art*; art critics deal with the unique creations of genius—they deal therefore with individual sculptors, painters, engravers and architects whose names are generally known from written sources or whose personalities at least are reputedly expressed in their creations. Like the political, military or ecclesiastical historian, the art-historian aims at recovering the thoughts and actions of individual personal agents.

An archæologist, as such, cannot hope to compete with him. As an archæologist he is confined to a world of abstractions, and his agents must be abstractions too. Yet, it must be insisted, archæology deals with the results of human actions, the embodiments of human thoughts and purposes. Whose? Who are the actors? Of course 'societies'—groups of individuals inspired by common purposes and needs and guided by a common tradition to their satisfaction.

Archæology studies indeed the results of human behaviour, but not so much the instinctive behaviour, specific to *Homo sapiens*—that would be a subject for zoology—but the patterns of behaviour learned from, and distinctive of, human societies. As animals, men seem to be omnivorous; what any individual man can enjoy and even digest is restricted to a remarkable extent by tastes and prejudices acquired from his society—his elders and fellows. The responses to other bodily impulses, such as defecation, are even more strictly regulated by social conventions. Distinctively human behaviour is still more patently social. To quote Emile Durkheim,[1] 'the system of signs I use to express my thoughts, the monetary system with which I pay my debts, the tools and the practices of my trade operate quite independently of any use I make of them. . . . We can choose the form of our houses no more than the cut of our clothes; the one is imposed on us to the same degree as the other' by social usage.

In particular men are born into this world equipped neither with bodily organs for securing food, avoiding danger and maintaining body temperature, nor with any specific instinct enabling them to remedy automatically these deficiencies. Man's biological success in the struggle for survival has been achieved by his capacity to make tools, clothes, houses, and in brief the whole contents of the archæological record. This

[1] E. Durkheim, *Les Règles de la méthode sociologique*, p. 6.

capacity has been learned, learned in the last resort by trial and error, but in almost every actual case from society through a cumulative social tradition. Mankind's technological progress and biological success would be inconceivable if each generation had had to find out for itself how to behave in the circumstances—the overwhelming majority—where innate instinct gave no precise guidance. Thanks to distinctively human means of communication with the aid of conventional symbols, each generation has been able to profit by the experience of previous generations, each individual from that of all members of his society, past and present.

A human child does not know instinctively how to use or make a tool as a caterpillar knows how to spin a cocoon: it has to be taught by its parents and elders, by the society into which it has been born. From the first standardized Abbevillian hand-axe half a million years ago, societies have been prescribing what tool to make, how to make it and the best material to make it of. Generation after generation has followed society's prescription and reproduced in thousands of instances the socially approved standard type. An archæological type is just that. Archæological phenomena can be grouped together as types just because results of private experience, of individual trial and error, have been communicated to other members of a society and adopted and replicated by them.

Of course each type began in the creative act of an individual, as the result of an unique discovery or invention. It became an archæological datum because, and only because, the discovery or invention was adopted and imitated by some society. An invention, however brilliant, that was never thus accepted and replicated would neither be recognizable by the archæologist nor for that matter of interest to the historian. On the other hand the most striking invention of a Watt or Edison is after all only a relatively trifling improvement on a complex of cognate inventions adopted and accumulated through social tradition over countless generations. To the steam-engine Watt added the slide-valve and the eccentric; he inherited from his own and earlier societies not only the Newcomen engine, but also precision lathes, steel, cast iron, an immense series of discoveries and inventions each in its time just as dramatic and revolutionary as his own contribution. At the same time he found at hand a body of skilled mechanics and artisans to execute his designs, a distributional system for assembling the requisite raw materials and parts and an assured market for his engines, in a word the social preconditions for the realization of his idea. Similarly an innovator in religion starts from a body of dogma and ritual, elaborated over many generations, as Buddha started from the Hinduism of the Brahmanas, and founds a new cult only if his innovations are espoused by a sufficiency of disciples.

The archæologist's restriction to abstract types is therefore after all not so serious a handicap as might appear. For types are just creations of individuals that have been approved, adopted and objectified by some society. The archæologist is then an historian, but an historian of culture. His agents are not concrete individuals, but abstract groups of persons who share a tradition to which each individual contributed. Community of tradition imposes on all members of the society in question a common pattern of behaviour. This must result in the production of standard types which, if they be artifacts, burial rites or remains of repasts, archæology can identify.

Indeed an archæological datum is a type just because it results from the behaviour pattern of a single society. It is a type too because it is an instance of an universal, the concrete expression and embodiment of a concept. This concept is—or was—objective in as much as it exists—or did exist—not in the maker's head alone, but in the heads of a society that transcended and outlasted each and all its members. In identifying types then the archæologist is really 're-enacting in his own mind' the thought of the agent (as Collingwood urged an historian must)—but not the subjective thought of an individual that might be distorted in its expression by incompetence or carelessness; what is thus recaptured and re-enacted is the objective thought entertained and realized by a society of persons.

The gravest defect of the archæological record is that so many of the types thus produced do not survive. It is indeed not quite true to say that behaviour does not fossilize. A great deal of learned human behaviour is expressed in actions that directly or indirectly leave a durable mark on the material world, as susceptible to scientific study and interpretation as the bony frames of extinct organisms. But just as the flesh, blood and sinews of the latter have failed to fossilize, so a still greater part of human behaviour has irrevocably vanished from the archæological record. Though certainly changes in the material world, the sound waves set up by human speaking by which information is conveyed and co-operative action organized, like the equally symbolic gestures and bodily movements, are wholly ephemeral. Many actions leading to more durable results have become quickly obliterated owing to the perishable material in which they were expressed. Save in very exceptional circumstances, all organic materials will completely decay in a few centuries. Bone, ivory, antler and shell may indeed last longer, and may even become fossilized and almost imperishable. Yet even bone in acid soils may be completely dissolved in fifty years unless it has been previously calcined—a process that, while preserving the substance, distorts or destroys its form.

Other materials—flesh, sinew, hide, wood and plant or animal fibres—hardly ever survive at all; nearly all objects made of these materials have perished. Thus scarcely any textile fabrics have survived. Not only wooden buildings and roofs of thatch or bark, but also the wooden vessels that furnished an early English farmhouse, geared machines, made wholly of timber in the late Middle Ages, and boats, vehicles and ploughs, still earlier made entirely of that material, are known from an infinitesimal number of actual specimens or deduced from indirect sources including pictures and written descriptions. A quite cursory glance at any ethnographic collection from the Polar regions, from North America, from the Pacific Islands, or from tropical Africa will disclose at once the frightful gap in the record thus caused. Not only food-stuffs, articles of clothing, houses and practical equipment, but also expressions of art and ritual have simply dropped out.

In exceptional circumstances, preserved on ice under barrows in the High Altai, in the wet mud of Alpine lakes, in the peat of North European bogs, in the sterile sands of the Egyptian desert or the Tarim basin, or in an old well that never dried up, intact leather articles like shoes, carpets and other textiles, complete carts and other products of carpentry and joinery, serve as a measure of our loss, but also help to fill the gap; for with due precautions the lesson of such finds can be generalized and used to complete the picture from other sites where similar types in durable materials alone survive. So too can less exceptional cases where for instance some textile fabric, impregnated with copper or iron salts, has been preserved on an axe-head or dagger-blade. Woodwork, though perished, often leaves observable traces. Refined excavation technique can recover the holes in the ground where posts once stood, and even the imprint of sleeper beams, and so recover the plan at least of a wooden building though no timber survives. Then, though the substance of wood, buried in the ground, may decay, the soil that replaces it will often differ in colour from the surrounding earth. By observing such differences Watelin and Woolley were enabled to trace the solid wheels and much of the structure of the hearses that conveyed to the tomb the early kings of Kish and Ur. By a further refinement Chinese excavators in 1951 succeeded in recovering the outlines of chariots with many-spoked wheels of the fourth or third century B.C.!

Apart from these exceptional cases, however, the archæological record consists all too often of battered pieces of stone, lumps of corroded metal, fragments of indestructible pottery, shapeless banks of earth and amorphous hollows in the ground—axe-heads without handles, whorls without spindles, hinges without doors and unfurnished rooms. But with proper precautions these gaps may partially be filled in by deductions from comparative ethnography as well as by the lucky finds mentioned above.

Finally objects normally fashioned of wood and given shapes proper to wood-carving may be copied in pottery or metal and then the copies disclose what the wood-carver could do. Thus the late Sir Ellis Minns could recognize the wood-work inspiration of the Scythian Beast Style even before the frozen wood from Pazyryk documented the models. Similar imitations of leather and textiles are recognizable. Sir John Myres has called '*skeuomorphs*' all objects, aping in one medium shapes proper to another. Often the ornamentation on a pot seems designed to enhance its

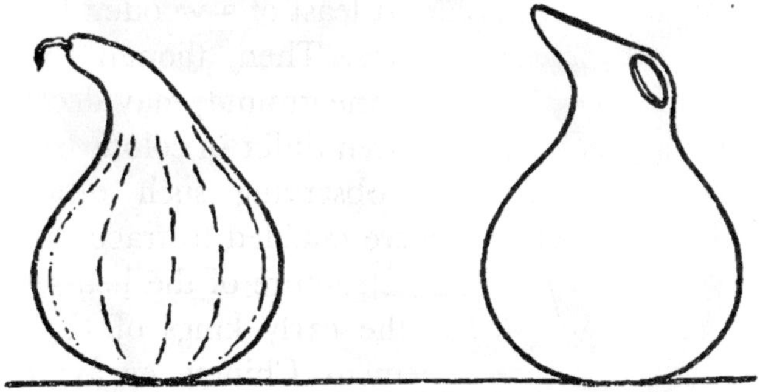

Gourd and pottery skeuomorph.

resemblance to a gourd in a string sling, to a stitched leather bottle or some other kind of container. Such patterns may be termed *skeuomorphic.* Skeuomorphism often gives us a glimpse into productive activities and artistic media of which no direct evidence survives.

Within the drastic limitations just indicated archæologists from observations on the external world try to decipher the standard behaviour patterns approved by past societies and to discover something of the fortunes of those societies and in particular their contributions to the pooled cultural tradition that we inherit. Though their aim is thus humanistic and historical, their data are more comparable to those studied by such natural sciences as zoology and botany. So archæological methods will approximate to those of the natural and inductive sciences. In the first place, the data must be classified. Archæological classification rests on three distinct bases; we might say that it

Bronze Vessels (1, 3, 5, 7) and clay copies (2, 4, 6, 8).

is three-dimensional, so that any archæological phenomenon could be located by three co-ordinates.

The first basis of classification is *functional*: what was the purpose of the act that produced the datum or the use of the latter? In practice this should generally mean 'What was the object for?' We accordingly sort out our data into functional groups; we put together for instance all adzes, daggers, razors, earrings, fields, dwelling-houses, granaries, castles, tombs, and so on. Then in each functional group we still recognize a vast number of different types. One reason for the observed differences may be age. Tools and weapons normally become more efficient as experience is gradually accumulated; the repetition of a traditional pattern by artists who have forgotten its meaning and lost the original inspiration results in progressive degeneration or distortion; notoriously fashions change with time. So we rearrange all our collections and inventory cards on a *chronological* basis. All adzes, attributable to one archæological period, will now be grouped with the daggers, razors, dwellings, tombs, etc., assigned to the same period. But within each chronological group thus formed we may still be faced with several different types of adze, dagger, razor, dwelling, grave. . . . We shall then observe on consulting the excavation reports that a given type of adze is often found with a given type of razor or dagger in a given type of tomb or dwelling, a second type of adze with a second type of dagger or razor in a second type of grave and so on. In the light of these *associations* we reclassify the contents of our chronological groups on a *chorological* basis.[1] And we remember from observations in the Balkans or other less industrialized parts of Europe, to say nothing of the unindustrialized regions of Africa or the Pacific, how fashions in dress and domestic architecture, burial rites and religious observances, even methods of wood-working or fighting diverge between different peoples, between, that is, groups united by common traditions but similarly distinguished from contemporary and neighbouring communities.

The methods adopted for ascertaining each of

[1] I have taken this rather ugly word from the Austrian; cf. O. Menghin, *Weltgeschichte der Steinzeit*, Vienna, 1931. I have not seen it previously used in English, but know no better equivalent.

the three co-ordinates—functional, chronological and chorological—will be discussed in separate chapters. But it is convenient to anticipate one common point. In practice it turns out that particular types of adze, dagger, razor and personal ornament are repeatedly found together in a particular type of grave and dwelling house under conditions implying simultaneous use.

Such a recurrent assemblage of archæological types is technically termed a *culture* while being found together with, in, or containing, is termed '*association*'. An obvious condition for the association of types is that they shall be in use or occupation at the same time. All types thus associated should then have the same chronological co-ordinate. But repeated association requires no less that they shall be used by the same society, that is by persons inspired by the same common tradition of wood-working, fighting, dress, domestic architecture and burial rites. That must be why all constituent items of a culture bear the same chorological co-ordinate. In fact it appears today that it is cultures, i.e. recurrent assemblages of types, and not isolated types, that have to be classified chronologically and studied. But this point has only been realized within the last quarter of the century.

CHAPTER TWO

How Young is Archæology?

A GLANCE at the story of archæology's beginnings and development will help the reader to understand concepts already mentioned. Indeed the terminology and some of the interpretative methods still normally employed must seem unbelievably inept unless one appreciates the historical conjunctures that evoked them. In fact archæology is a recent and still raw recruit to the ranks of the scientific disciplines. It is rather a hybrid, uneasily straddling the unstable frontier between natural sciences and humanities. Actually it has two roots: one goes back to the precursors of Natural History, the other to the classical humanism of the Renaissance.[1]

Objects now recognized as human products were first studied by naturalists along with other phenomena of the non-human environment. Thus stone celts, so enormously common throughout North-western Europe, have been traditionally regarded as

[1] This chapter is a summary of my contribution to *Science, Medicine and History*, ed. E. Ashworth Underwood, London, 1952, where references are given. For further details, see also Glynn E. Daniel, *A Hundred Years of Archaeology*, London, 1950.

thunderbolts and are still so regarded by many peasantries today; last century they were popularly termed *pierres à foudre* in France and *Donnerkeil* in Germany. Learnedly labelled *keraunia*, they provided a theme for erudite but inconclusive discussions among schoolmen and antiquaries till Mercati, Curator of the Vatican Botanical Gardens between 1560 and 1590, learned of the stone hatchets used by the aborigines of the recently discovered New World. Anticipating the comparative method of interpretation (discussed here in Chapter Three), he explained keraunia as really the axe-blades once used by prehistoric Europeans. In the same way Scottish vitrified forts (ramparts of stone, laced with timber that becoming ignited were reduced to a fused mass like slag) were mistaken for products of vulcanism and hence curiously examined by geologists. Williams first recognized their human origin in 1777, but the unintentional nature of their 'vitrifaction' was not established till 1935.

Mediæval pharmacology had also contributions to make. The prescription of 'powdered mummy' and 'giants' bones' encouraged the collection of ancient skeletons and bones of unusual size. Curative virtue in kidney troubles, superstitiously ascribed to 'nephrite' (a greenstone), seems responsible for the oldest extant scientific account of a prehistoric tomb. For a megalithic long cist, exposed at Cocherel near Evreux in 1685, contained a fine nephrite axe and, presumably for this reason, was faithfully observed by the local doctor and eventually described in Montfaucon's *L'Antiquité expliquée et représentée en figures*, published in 1719.

It was, however, those geologists engaged in founding the palæontological and glaciological branches of the science who played a leading role in moulding a new science of archæology. In 1715 Bagford accepted, though he misinterpreted, the association of a flint 'hand-axe', certainly shaped by man, with the skeleton of an 'elephant' (? mammoth) near Gray's Inn Lane. Then in 1797 John Frere described flint implements found in undisturbed strata with bones of extinct animals at Hoxne as 'weapons of war fabricated and used by a people who had not the use of metals' and attributable to 'a very remote period indeed, even beyond that of the present world'. Dean Buckland had exposed a fossilized human skeleton wearing a bracelet of mammoth ivory and embedded among the remains of extinct animals in Paviland Cave, South Wales, in 1823. But on theological grounds Buckland refused to believe his own eyes. Soon, however, Belgian and French geologists detected so many evidences of human industry in cave deposits associated with an extinct fauna that the existence of antediluvian man became hard to deny. More decisive, however, were the researches of Boucher de Perthes, a customs official of Abbeville. From ancient terrace gravels of the Somme, laid down in an early period of the Pleistocene, he collected a large series of chipped flints that he claimed as products of human handiwork. French savants rejected his arguments, as set forth in *Antiquités celtiques et antédiluviennes* in 1847. It was not till the English antiquaries and geologists, John Evans, Falconer and Prestwich, visited Abbeville in 1859 and inspected the sites and collections, that the authenticity of Boucher de Perthes' hand-axes was admitted. The existence of Pleistocene man was thereby established in 1859.

But in that same year the publication of *The Origin*

of Species and the consequent triumph of the Theory of Evolution or 'transformism' broke down the barriers between Natural History and Human History. The naturalist tradition in archæology could thus unite with the humanist tradition that had been growing up and to which we must now turn back.

The humanist tradition began with the revival of interest in classical learning at the Renaissance. Architects and artists turned for inspiration to the visible ruins of Roman and Greek buildings and temples, to statues, mosaics and painted vases. The surviving monuments were described and illustrated in handsome atlases. Soon students of Classical Antiquity sought to supplement the examples visible above ground by uncovering more and ransacked ancient tombs for 'Etruscan vases'. After 1738 extensive if disorderly excavations at Herculaneum and Pompeii, cities buried by the eruption of Vesuvius in 80, recaptured the daily life of classical cities with a vividness and freshness that no written description could rival. Nevertheless the prime motive in these excavations, as in the earlier explorations of the dilettanti at the Renaissance, had been the collection and recovery of *objets d'art* and perhaps also inscriptions to supplement the traditional written sources of ancient history. The French foundation of 1716 bears the name, 'Académie des inscriptions et belles lettres'.

At the beginning of the nineteenth century this sort of archæological exploration and collecting, which had been recovering some of the concrete remains of Greco-Roman civilization, was extended to other older civilizations that had hitherto been mere names in Classical and Biblical literature. When Napoleon sailed for Egypt in 1798 he was accompanied not only by naturalists, but also by archæologists who were to record the celebrated monuments of his Empire's new province. And record they did, magnificently, though the new province was never France's. In the sequel Champollion's decipherment of the hieroglyphic inscription on the Rosetta Stone opened a whole new volume of literary records extending written history backwards over two thousand five hundred years. The parallel exploration of the Tigris-Euphrates valley was initiated in 1842 by the excavations at Nineveh undertaken by Botta, the French consul at Mosul.

It is irrelevant here to pursue further the story of archæology in the Near East beyond noting two points. In the Oriental field archæology has always been more closely linked up with the earlier or Oriental chapters of orthodox Ancient History than with the later or Classical chapters. Even in the present century in a standard text-book like Bury's *History of Greece*, mention of archæological documents was carefully confined to a couple of detached sections that the student knew he could safely ignore for examination purposes. No history of Egypt or Babylonia ever dismissed tomb paintings, statues, stelae and boundary stones so summarily. On the other hand archæological exploration remained for a long time a hunt for tablets and other inscribed documents, for cylinder seals, scarabs and *objets d'art* and an effort to expose monumental structures calculated to impress patrons. Even in Greece sacred and public buildings, figured bronzes, painted vases, gems, coins and inscriptions were the proper subdivisions of Classical Archæology. Phenomena that did not fall under these heads like domestic architecture, craftsmen's tools, mills, household pottery, were officially frowned on till workers trained in

European prehistory began to take a hand in Greece, Egypt and Mesopotamia after 1890.

For it was in lands where written sources began late, in the last-acquired provinces of the Roman Empire and beyond the Empire's frontiers, that archæology came to be not a mere illustration of written history, but an autonomous source of history with its own proper methods and concepts. Of course the glamour of Rome had guaranteed the study of the Empire's monuments right to its frontiers in Britain, South Germany and Hungary as much as in metropolitan Italy. Nor did English, French and North European antiquaries fail to study their native monuments of the Christian period—abbeys, castles, manors, tombs—with as much sympathy and perhaps in a more scientific spirit.

But with the Gothic Revival and the Romantic Movement Englishmen, Frenchmen and Germans turned their gaze beyond the alien invaders to seek the monuments of their own Celtic and Teutonic ancestors, while in the remoter lands beyond the Empire's frontiers the memory of pagan Vikings and Slavs likewise stirred the antiquarian imagination. So Aubrey and Stukeley in England described Avebury and Stonehenge; country gentlemen in Britain and on the Continent dug into barrows; the 'dolmens' of Brittany were searched for Druidic relics; Viking howes and the still older Giants' Tombs were opened in the search for treasures that Beowulf did not find. The results were not spectacular—rude stone burial chambers, simple tools of iron, bronze or stone, unpainted hand-made vases and no inscriptions. But these poor relics were invested with a sentimental value and a patriotic appeal. By the beginning of last century quite substantial collections of such antiques had been assembled in royal or private museums along with miscellaneous curiosities. They had to be arranged and their arrangement evoked the first distinctively archæological classification.

In France and the British Isles indeed allusions in classical writers were invoked to confer a spurious historicity on ancient native artifacts; if not 'Roman', they could be catalogued as 'Gaulish', 'Belgic', 'Ancient British' or 'Druidic'. In Sweden and Denmark no such respectable names were available. Yet the soil of Scandinavia had yielded a quite exceptionally rich harvest of stone and bronze implements, and rude stone tombs that could not be attributed to the historical Danes and Swedes of Christian times. How were they to be labelled? C. J. Thomsen, appointed in 1816 the first curator of the National Museum of Northern Antiquities in Copenhagen, had to arrange for exhibition an exceptionally rich collection of relics, derived in part from systematic excavation. He decided to group together such things as had been used together, that is in the same period. But none of the antiquities from pagan times were dated by king's reigns or other references to events recorded in written chronicles; they were preliterate. Now Thomsen, like Lucretius, believed that men had once used stone alone for tools and weapons, later stone and bronze, and later still iron too. This sequence provided the basis for a purely archæological arrangement—the celebrated *Three Ages*. All relics that were found associated exclusively with stone tools and weapons and such graves as contained them were assigned to the 'Stone Age'. Any type ever found with bronze artifacts but never with iron was labelled 'Bronze Age'. Whatever types were ever associated with iron, were then left to fill the 'Pagan Iron Age'.

Between 1835 and 1865 stratigraphical observations had confirmed Thomsen's *a priori* sequence and shown that it was valid outside Scandinavia, and thereafter it was gradually adopted all over Europe as the naturalist tradition began to blend with the humanist. Their union demanded one modification. The recognition of Pleistocene man showed that Thomsen's first division must be enormously longer than the others. Discoveries in the Swiss lakes, beginning with the exceptionally dry winter of 1853–4, emphasized the immense contrast between the equipment and way of life of Pleistocene man and those of his successors. So the Stone Age was divided into two, christened by Lubbock, in 1865, 'Palæolithic' and 'Neolithic' respectively.

Thomsen's classification was logical and consistent; it was based on a single, easily determinable criterion —the *material of the principal cutting tools and weapons*. It purported to give, and did give, a succession of technological periods of indefinite length which followed one another in the same order all over Europe; it never claimed for them the universal validity of geological ages or historical eras. No one for instance doubted that the Bronze Age had begun much earlier in Egypt than in Denmark. But for the distinction between Palæolithic and Neolithic three separate criteria were proposed: (1) technological, the edging of implements exclusively by chipping as contrasted with grinding and polishing; (2) economic, dependence on wild food as against farming; and (3) geological, association with a Pleistocene or a recent fauna respectively. The last criterion had the effect of identifying the archæological period, Palæolithic, with the geological period Pleistocene, which for geologists ends simultaneously all over the Earth.

Of course it was believed that the three criteria coincided, but subsequent investigations showed that they did not; in Europe a long interval elapsed between the end of the Pleistocene and the foundation of the first farming villages. Some few writers still cling to the geological criterion and label everything post-Pleistocene 'Neolithic'. Since 1921 archæologists have as a whole adopted the economic criterion for the Neolithic and have rather reluctantly accepted a 'Mesolithic period' to accommodate post-Pleistocene hunters who grew no corn and kept no cows or sheep.

Thomsen had created a purely archæological classification, but inspired essentially by the humanist tradition. Fifty years later Gabriel de Mortillet proposed, and won considerable acceptance for, a subdivision of Thomsen's 'ages' modelled on geological classifications and symbolizing the union of the humanist and naturalist traditions. De Mortillet was given charge of the prehistoric section of the Musée des Antiquités nationales at S. Germain, founded by Napoleon III to illustrate the *Histoire de César* he planned to write. His training had been in natural history rather than the classics, and he modelled his arrangement of the collections at S. Germain on the well-established geological system. He planned to divide up Thomsen's ages as geologists divided their eras. In geology the order of periods is determined by stratigraphy in the first instance. But once observation at a few sites has thus established a sequence of 'type-fossils', each distinctive of a period in the succession, the occurrence of a type-fossil in a rock anywhere is taken as an index of its geological age. The periods thus defined are named after regions where the characteristic fossil-bearing deposits have been first recognized or are exceptionally well developed (Permian from Perm, the former 'Government' near the Urals, Devonian from Devon, and so on).

On these principles de Mortillet divided the Stone Age into six periods, each defined by a distinctive assemblage of types. Their order was allegedly based on stratigraphical observations made in France and Switzerland, and each was named after a site where the distinctive types were supposed to be well represented—Chelles, le Moustier, Solutré, la Madelaine, Robenhausen. Divisions of the Bronze Age and the pre-Roman Iron Age, named on the same principles, followed.

In this scheme de Mortillet formulated a distinctively archæological method for establishing archæological chronology and a convenient nomenclature. It is a relatively trivial fault that in arranging his sequence, he was sometimes guided rather by typology—an hypothetical evolution of his type-fossils—than by observed stratigraphical succession; consequent errors could be, and eventually were, corrected. The system's gravest defect, that made it a stumbling-block impeding further development, lay elsewhere. Flushed with the recent triumph of transformism, de Mortillet presented each period, like the Age of which it was a division, as an evolutionary stage through which every society must pass; the succession supposedly established in France was apparently generalized; its divisions, named after French sites, were raised to the status of periods of world prehistory, on a level with Cambrian, Jurassic and the other divisions of geological time.

Probably no one, not even the system's author, seriously attributed any such value to its later periods; it was obviously ridiculous to talk of a Larnaudian period in Egypt or a Marnian in Greece.

But de Mortillet's divisions of the Old Stone Age were taken literally as periods of geological time and general stages in cultural evolution. As exploration extended to other parts of Europe and then to other continents, the assemblages there found were forcibly squeezed into this narrow frame. Even when it became obvious that a newly found assemblage lacked all the type-fossils that characterized de Mortillet's periods in France, it was called after the French period that occupied the same relative position in the French sequence as it was supposed to occupy in the local sequence. Most prehistorians in the U.S.S.R. till 1950 used de Mortillet's terms in this chronological sense and so do a few prehistorians elsewhere. But such a usage caused frightful confusion, since other writers employed the same name in a quite different sense as the chorological co-ordinate of the assemblage of types. The fact is that de Mortillet, like many naturalists of his day, looked upon the development of human culture as a continuation of organic evolution and regarded both as unilinear. His system accordingly has the effect of an attempt to confine human history within the categories of natural history. The correction had to come from the side of the humanists.

Not even in France did the heirs of that tradition accept de Mortillet's unilineal evolution. For Bertand the transition from the Stone Age to the Bronze Age in Europe was not due to any development on the spot, but to an invasion by 'Aryans' who subdued or exterminated 'the nameless peoples' (*peuples innommés*) of the Stone Age. Indeed de Mortillet himself helped to show that one assemblage of type-fossils could be used to define, not only a period of archæological time in France, but also a nation known to written history; the types, characterizing his 'Marnian' in France and Switzerland, proved in Italy to be distinctive of the Gauls, known to have descended from that direction. It was, however, in Northern Europe and especially in Germany, where a new spirit of nationalism had been growing up since 1870 and where few Palæolithic finds had been made, that archæologists first came to see clearly that assemblages of type fossils might characterize not only distinct periods of time, but also distinct nations or tribes within a single period. And it was German prehistorians who came to term such recurrent assemblages of type-fossils 'Kulturen'—a word unhappily translated into English as 'cultures', used in a partitive sense, but used in much this sense by ethnographers too! The recognition of the third basis of archæological classification, called, in Chapter One, chorological, marks a fresh era in prehistory. It was formulated explicitly before the end of the nineteenth century by Gustav Kossinna, a philologist and Germanist who turned from the humanities to archæology: 'Sharply defined archæological culture-provinces coincide at all times with quite definite peoples or tribes; cultural regions are ethnic regions, culture groups are peoples.'

In the present century such conceptions spread gradually to England and Scandinavia. But to the Palæolithic Age such a chorological cross-classification, apart from hints by Obermaier in 1908 and Breuil in 1912, was not systematically applied till 1923 when it was formulated explicitly by Menghin. In France it was first in 1933 that Peyrony split the old Aurignacian into two distinct but partly contemporary cultures. In 1938 the new conception was applied to the whole Upper Palæolithic by Garrod. Unfortunately some of de Mortillet's period names have still been retained to designate the new chorological divisions. In reading a book today the reader must look at the date to find out what Aurignacian or Azilian means!

CHAPTER THREE

What is 'the Archæological Record'?

THE archæological record does not consist of isolated monuments rising gaunt and empty from the level field nor yet of stray bits of stone, metal or earthenware turned up by a plough or a bull-dozer. Such are only potential archæological documents; however carefully planned or collected, such would hardly be amenable to archæological classification. By themselves they would scarcely be reducible even to types. It would often be hard to determine their function, still harder to estimate their archæological age, never possible to assign them to one society rather than another. It is only because we find lost trifles and scraps in house floors, mortuary offerings in graves, or relics in some other kind of context that they can become archæological data. You will remember that the nut from my car on page 3 became embedded in the roadway, naturally with similar bits of junk and doubtless eventually sealed by a fresh layer of tar and would therefore be found by the Fuegian archæologist 'in a context'. So I thoughtfully buried a sardine tin in the hole on Esher Common.

It is nearly always association with other phenomena that gives a first clue as to the use, the age and the chorological attribution of a potential datum. But age at least may sometimes be inferred from position in a geological deposit or a layer of peat. And once a type has been classified by the aid of its context, further specimens of the same type, even when found in isolation, can be assigned their place and interpreted. Scottish museums contained over a hundred elaborately carved stone balls collected in various counties without significant context. Their age and use was a matter of sheer speculation till a fine example was unearthed at Skara Brae in Orkney and the Neolithic age of that settlement determined. Now, though their use is still unknown, their chronological co-ordinate is fixed and they can be used to define the extent of the Rinyo-Clacton culture.

The archæological context should disclose *association*. When a group of types are found together under circumstances suggesting contemporary use they are said to be *associated*. Mere physical juxtaposition does not guarantee association. A number of stone implements may turn up together in a gravel pit dug in a Pleistocene river channel. The gravel consists of debris picked up by the river and its tributaries anywhere in its large catchment area and promiscuously dumped together where the force of the current abated. There is no guarantee that all the implements included in the gravel had been made or used together or even in the same geological period; some might have been washed out of older gravels laid down millennia earlier and then mixed with others made and used on the surface of those older gravels. Braidwood[1] describes such a fortuitous collection as an *aggregate*.

[1] R. Braidwood, 'Terminology in Prehistory', *Human Origins: Selected Readings*, II (mimeo), University of Chicago, 1945.

Association on the other hand can best be illustrated by the following examples: the relics trodden into the earthen floor of a house and the house itself—in practice the house plan—constitute an assemblage of associated types; so do the mortuary offerings accompanying a single interment together with the form of the tomb, the burial rite and any traces of peculiarities of the corpse. The contents of hoards—that is to say groups of coins or other portable relics found together in a jar or chest or under conditions suggesting that they had been packed together in some such way, must likewise be accepted as associated, but reservations must be made in respect of the exact significance to be attached to 'contemporary use'. In the case of coin hoards, though individual coins may range in date over a century or two, it may be assumed that all were current in the lifetime of the miser who hoarded them. On the other hand many collections of bronze objects comprise old and battered pieces; they seem in fact to consist largely of scrap metal collected for re-smelting. It cannot then be inferred that their constituents had been in contemporary use as swords, axes, razors or safety-pins. Similar ambiguity often infects votive offerings deposited in a temple, a sacred cave, or a bog, and the grave-goods in a collective tomb, used for several generations.

Association is essential for determining the chronological co-ordinate of any archæological datum. It is still more crucial for determining its chorological co-ordinate. The same types often recur together in a number of deposits—not only in many graves of the same cemetery or in several houses in the same village, but also in several distinct cemeteries or villages or in hoards, scattered over a continuous area. Such recurrent assemblages of types, or groups of types repeatedly found associated, constitute what are termed 'cultures' as stated on page 16, but only provided the assemblages illustrate more than one aspect of human behaviour. A recurrent assemblage of stone tools, never found in any recognizable type of dwelling or grave, nor even associated with broken bones of game indicative of a distinctive selection of menus, should not be termed a culture, but an *industry*.

In defining a culture in this way three points should be noted.

(1) Not all the types to be assigned to a culture need recur in every assemblage constituent of that culture; we should not expect to find all types in each house or in each grave, nor even in every village or cemetery. But to qualify for inclusion in the culture's content any type should be represented in at least two representative sites and by more than one example.

(2) On the other hand many types, indicative of highly significant cultural behaviour, recur in varied assemblages over a vast area and throughout a long range of time. For instance, all farmers in Europe and Western Asia from the earliest Neolithic times cultivated emmer and barley, and till 500 B.C. nearly all ground their corn to flour on saddle querns of very similar type. Such things are therefore useless for classifying cultures though of prime importance in describing them. Other phenomena, less significant in themselves—specialized types of flint knife, of hand-made vase, or of safety-pin are found to be confined to a single horizon in several stratified sites and to a limited continuous area. Such phenomena have been used since de Mortillet as *type fossils* to define archæological periods and cultures. Any assemblage containing one

or more of the type-fossils recognized as distinctive of culture A is assigned to culture A subject to the reservation indicated in paragraph (3). Assemblages in different layers or at other sites in which the foregoing type-fossils are missing and in which some of them are replaced by different types will be assigned to a new culture, B, even though many types be common to both A and B assemblages.

(3) A type-fossil distinctive of culture B may turn up sporadically associated with a predominantly A assemblage. Such strays, provided they really are strays, i.e. are relatively very rare in A assemblages in contrast with their high frequency in B, do not invalidate the distinction established between the two cultures, but are held to indicate some sort of relation, for instance, trade, between them.

It will be seen from the foregoing that the archæological concept of culture is largely statistical. The larger the number of closed finds in which the same types are associated and the more types thus associated, the less likely is the association to be fortuitous, the greater the probability of an organic coherence between the types as products of one common pattern of behaviour. It is part of the archæologist's business to discover this pattern and thus disclose the inner connexion between data that in the raw appear as isolated fragments. As will be shown in more detail in Chapter Six an archæologist does not conceive a culture as 'a thing of threads and patches', a mechanical aggregate of 'traits', but as an organic whole. Least of all is an archæological culture characterized by a few type-fossils. Yet these type-fossils are the sole marks by which a culture can be recognized and distinguished from another.

Admittedly the conception of type-fossils has been made a decisive instrument in archæological classification. Evidently too this use rests upon assumptions, though these are rarely formulated. They should be frankly stated. An archæological datum is a type precisely because it is the result of an invention or thought that has been published, approved, adopted and repeated by members of a society so that a social tradition prescribes both what to do and how to do it. That is itself an assumption, indeed a postulate, but the use of type-fossils involves a further assumption.

It assumes that it is highly improbable that the discovery, invention, composition or innovation embodied in the type-fossil should have been made and adopted independently by two or more societies, separated by no great distance in space or time from one another. For archæological classification it is in practice not necessary to rule out the possibility of two or more independent inventions if the whole of the earth's surface and archæological time be surveyed. For that extension of purview, by enormously increasing the number of societies that might have happened on the innovation enhances correspondingly the probability that more than one did. In interpreting the classified archæological record this very issue arises, but for its classification we can narrow down the number of opportunities considerably.

An archæological type or assemblage of types is a message from the past. Now communication engineers work on the principle that information conveyed by a message is inversely proportional to its probability. Applying their rule to archæological messages we see that the significance of a type as a type-fossil is proportionate to its improbability. Unluckily there is no reliable criterion for determining that by inspection. Still less can cultural probability be measured by a mathematical formula. A few hints can be deduced from general principles. An archæological type is defined for descriptive purposes by technique and form; it may also be a vehicle for decoration though patterns and style may be treated as themselves types. Material is limited first by what is available to the actor society and secondly by the latter's accumulation of scientific lore. It is thus a useful index of a society's rank in an economic and technological hierarchy and may be decisive in determining the type's chorological co-ordinate, but with the limited choice permitted any material is comparatively probable. So too the techniques for working flint, for manufacturing metal articles, for disposing of deceased kinsmen or decorating a wall with paintings are strictly limited so that no one is highly improbable; a piece of flint may in practice be flaked (1) by bashing it on a fixed anvil, by hitting it (2) with a hammer-stone or (3) with a baton, by pressure (4) on an anvil or (5) with a punch. Though some of these methods might be subdivided, some must be combined with others so that the probability of any one would be as high as 1 in 5 at least. The variety of forms that can be given even to a simple tool, of plans for the lay out of a house, and of receptacles for ashes or corpses is very much greater. Function of course imposes definite limitations on the shape of an axe or the plan of a farm and material too restricts the designer's freedom. Nonetheless a surprisingly wide scope is left for the exercise of unfettered imagination, and the number of often seemingly arbitrary variations on an axe-head or a farm-house that were socially standardized and thus made types is rather alarming to the novice though an immense asset for archæological classification. The exceptional prominence attached to pottery in archæology lies in the fact that, clay being completely plastic, leaves the potter theoretically at liberty to mould it to whatever shape fancy may suggest. Any given shape is therefore in itself relatively improbable and this improbability can be multiplied by that of the technique used and again by that of the ornament yielding a quite fantastic negative logarithm.

Such theoretical considerations are not really reliable guides to the probability or the reverse of human actions. In estimating the significance of a type-fossil an archæologist will be wise to rely on the observed frequency or rarity of the type in assemblages that are spatially or chronologically well separated. The results are sometimes surprising. For instance, the tanged and barbed arrow-head, commonly regarded as the standard type, in stone has never been found in the British Isles with an assemblage, classed on other grounds as Neolithic, and is surprisingly rare throughout Eurasia save on the Atlantic coasts. Flint arrow-heads of this seemingly banal form are therefore confidently accepted as type-fossils of the Bronze Age in the British Isles while the rare specimens found in Scandinavia or Central Europe are suspected of being imports from farther west or local copies of such. Archæologists' confidence in their value has not been shaken by the surprising discovery of missile points, indistinguishable from the best British Bronze Age arrow-heads in a Solutrean context in Spain!

It will be seen from the general principles summarized above and from the example just given that it is comparatively trivial aspects of social behaviour that arm the archæologist with his most serviceable type-fossils; historically the use of the bow is far more significant than the precise shape of the missile shot from it. An unfortunate consequence of the importance necessarily attached, in constructing the archæological record, to type-fossils and of the latters' peculiarities is that most pages in text-books or learned journals have to be devoted to erudite discussions about the minutiæ of ceramic ornamentation, of styles of capitals, or of the orientation of corpses. The layman and the literary historian thus get the impression that archæologists are completely engrossed in making ever finer distinctions between flint knives, drinking cups, eikons and latch-keys. Of course that sort of thing is the archæologist's first business; but for that there would be no archæological record at all, only collections of curios and catalogues of picturesque ruins.

But such trifles, we repeat, do not constitute the archæological record; they merely provide a frame to support a pattern of more vital tissue. The substance of the record is constituted by the houses of the living and the dead with the evidence of daily activities and solemn rituals they supply, the craftsmen's tools through which the practical science of past ages was applied, the carvings or paintings that directly express ideas and ideals. If their arrangement and classification depend upon the most variable and improbable playthings of fashion, that does not exempt or preclude archæologists from studying and presenting the permanent contributions made by the age and by the society that in each case is defined for them by its most ephemeral fancies.

CHAPTER FOUR

What was it for?

THE first basis of archæological classification is functional (page 14). Every archæological datum is the result of an act of man, an act done normally for the satisfaction of some socially approved human purpose. Quite a high proportion of our data are actually the instruments with which such purposes were to be satisfied. There would indeed be no archæological record at all but for the fact that to satisfy nearly all his needs Man has to make and use tools—extracorporeal organs. Rabbits make quite substantial and durable 'changes in the external world', but there is no archæology of rabbits since they make their burrows entirely with bodily limbs and organs.

But just because they are human, the purposes, expressed in archæological data and to be deciphered therefrom by archæology, are capricious and almost infinitely variable. The behaviour of rabbits or sheep, despite insignificant individual deviations, is extraordinarily uniform. It could be explained—perhaps rather superficially—by reference to a strictly limited set of biological needs, common to all members of the species and satisfied by an almost equally restricted range of innate instinctive reactions. All members of our species too, as animals, doubtless share a stock of common needs—for food, shelter, sexual intercourse, defecation and so on. But the satisfaction of the most 'animal' needs is not specific as it is with sheep or rabbits. Even what a man will eat and can in fact digest, is socially determined, determined that is by the training he or she has received from society. Many Englishmen would be made physically sick by eating pony or frog if they were told what they were eating!

Nor are human needs limited by these instinctive biological appetites. Human societies have been constantly developing new needs and these vary from society to society. For their satisfaction societies have developed appropriate instruments that may leave a substantial imprint on the archæological record but are themselves still more variable. Since the sixteenth century European societies have developed a passion for tobacco-smoking and an impressive paraphernalia of pipes, pouches, ash-trays, spittoons, smokers' companions and so on now enriches the archæological record. Melanesians and Polynesians on the other hand are devoted to betel-chewing and present archæologists with an equally elaborate and varied apparatus for the ceremonial satisfaction of this socially recognized need! No appeal to 'universal laws of animal behaviour' nor to 'the constitution of the human mind' would enable an archæologist of the Sixth millennium A.D. to unravel the purpose of a Trobriand betel-box or an Oxford tobacco-jar. But as each is a type fashioned to meet the demand of a whole society, even if all written or oral tradition be lost, he will always have the chance of finding the puzzling type in a context that will reveal its function. For the latter after all is the satisfaction of a purpose that is in practice attainable.

But contemporary and past societies have entertained desires and sanctioned purposes for the satisfaction of which no means have been discovered even by modern science—for the indefinite prolongation of life or for foreknowledge of the future, for instance. Apparently in the hope of attaining such ends, they have made durable and substantial 'changes in the material world' indeed as monumental and lasting as the pyramids of Egypt! In so far as no act, however deep its imprint on the archæological record, is known to have secured to its performer immortality or even precise knowledge as to which horse would win the Spring Stakes on the morrow, no two societies have agreed on the precise procedure to be followed for the attainment of such ends. So it is impossible for an archæologist to deduce with complete assurance precisely what end the surviving result of any particular futile act or piece of behaviour were designed to serve.

Again many societies have imagined means for, or at least short-cuts to, the attainment of socially desired ends that are in fact perfectly attainable, but not by those methods. I refer of course to various 'superstitious' practices and magic rites prescribed by different societies to ensure success in fishing, a good harvest, the cure of this or that curable or incurable disease and all the other vain imaginings of that ilk. As in the long run none is empirically justified by success, there has been no universal agreement as to precisely what 'superstitious behaviour' would be appropriate to securing each desired result. Though in some cases, for instance in fertility rites, comparative ethnography discloses widespread but quite abstract similarities, the concrete details of ritual behaviour diverge enormously from group to group. And it is the concrete acts alone that can leave fossil traces in the archæological record. Though archæologists have learned from ethnographers that perfectly efficient fishing tackle is liable to be supplemented by quite futile magical appurtenances, that knowledge would not suffice to interpret say a Fijian cuttle-fish lure unless it happened to be found in a context pointing very explicitly to the catching of cuttle-fish!

Nor would such interpretations in terms of ulterior purposes be necessarily correct after all; they may quite well be *ex post facto* rationalizations. Perhaps men really do some actions for their own sake and not as means to the satisfaction of some remoter need! Men do things because they have learned to feel they ought to do them, because society expects them to do so, because they have become habituated to so doing or just because they like it! Building a cathedral or a temple is in itself an act of merit, what society thinks ought to be done. In our Middle Ages nobles and merchants, patricians and artisans participated as volunteers in erecting a cathedral; in the third millennium B.C. all citizens from the 'king' down were proud to carry bricks for a Sumerian temple. Such conduct was prescribed by society as a duty; the citizens acted so because they felt they ought—if you will, to satisfy a religious or moral need.

It would be quite irrelevant if the city fathers justify the expenditure on the ground that by pleasing God, it would ensure a good harvest or commercial success. Such subjective motives lie beyond the archæologists' ken. The archæologist would not be a better historian if he sought to depict a temple or a cathedral as a mistaken and costly substitute for an irrigation canal!

Again an artist gets æsthetic satisfaction from painting a picture, not from contemplating the finished product, still less from selling it. If an individual artist does paint just to make money, that would be an irrelevant deviation from the socially approved motivation. So too a woman will wear jewellery to gratify her æsthetic sense or her vanity, not primarily to ensnare a man. Once again it is the sort of thing expected of her; the best people in her society wear jewellery. That much archæology can recognize, but no more.

Still more obviously men play golf or backgammon because they like doing so, or at least because it is the thing to do, but not to secure any ulterior result. British golf-courses today, pre-Columbian ball-courts in America, the dice from the Bronze Age Indus cities and Iron Age villages like Glastonbury must be interpreted in the light of this admission.

Archæologists would be well advised to admit that men often act for the sake of acting. Societies prescribe patterns of such disinterested action and invest them and their results with values. Societies prescribe rites and ceremonial behaviour, styles of art and ornament, fashions of dress and personal adornment, games and sports. All these may leave recognizable impressions on the archæological record. Their results are then significant indications of the values recognized by the society in question. Utility is not the only value admitted by any society. Why pretend in defiance of all observation that all rational human behaviour, save the satisfaction of the animal's basic needs, must be a means to satisfy those needs? Why assume that the answer to our question 'What is it for?' must be framed in such utilitarian terms? A representation or a design is the result of artistic activity. It approximates to, and to that extent reveals, the standard of beauty approved by a specific society. If beyond that it were a means to an ulterior end that is certainly unknowable and probably irrelevant. A personal ornament is 'for' adorning the person and nothing else. It is again historically significant as illustrating the tastes of a given society. At the same time it may disclose the motive for some economic activity—for trade, for industry. Indeed sacred rites and edifices, games and sports, art and ornament, far from being merely means to economic ends, supply ends for practical economic activities.

For descriptive purposes the monuments and relics resulting from these ritual, sportive or artistic activities may be relegated to the category of 'Spiritual Culture'. Of course no society can indulge in ceremonies, games and ornaments, unless it can produce enough food and shelter to maintain itself and to enable its members to produce and rear children. To this extent 'spiritual culture' can legitimately be called a 'superstructure' supported by the productive system.

Fortunately therefore the bulk of the archæological record falls within the domain, tritely termed 'Material Culture'. Most archæological data, that is to say, result from actions directed to the satisfaction of needs that *Homo sapiens* shares with other animals. Of course such satisfaction is in all cases sought or obtained in a distinctively human way and in particular with the aid of extracorporeal organs—artefacts, not organically attached to the human body nor yet produced from it like a spider's web. With this qualification it may be said that at least a large proportion of our relics and monuments served, albeit often very indirectly and in a roundabout way, to the procurement of food, shelter, warmth, protection against foes, human and non-human, and hygiene. These are attainable ends, and the means to the attainment, though very varied, are finite in number. That number has been gradually reduced by a slow process of 'natural selection' of the most efficient means.

The foregoing needs, being common to all men, albeit in a very generalized form, the socially approved and standardized instruments for their satisfaction exhibit a generic, albeit very abstract, similarity. Most societies want to chop things and to dig in the ground. Hence chopping and digging tools, despite an enormous range of variations, are generally recognizable, and therefore classifiable archæologically. The trouble is that contemporary archæologists generally work with bull-dozers and tooth-brushes and need never have handled or even seen an adze or a pick. Luckily, when the functional classification of relics began a century ago, manual tools were still familiar even in industrialized Britain so that their less efficient precursors could in many cases be safely identified.

Similarly, though invisible enemies are now generally killed in bulk by pressing buttons, a century ago swords, lances and helmets were still employed in actual warfare, and the lethal use of the ornate weapons, now paraded only on state occasions, is generally understood today. Hence our predecessors, like General Pitt Rivers, had no difficulty in tracing and transmitting to us the pedigree of many tools and weapons right back to the Old Stone Age. The contemporary archæologist has thus inherited a reliable functional classification for a long range of his types.

In drawing up this classification archæologists have constantly and profitably appealed to ethnography and folk-lore. There exist today or have existed quite recently communities that are, or have been, effectively untouched by the Industrial Revolution, whose industries are unmechanized, some of whom indeed are still unacquainted with any metal. They are indeed living fossils; observations on their equipment, on their industrial processes and on their standard of living provide the most illuminating means for reclothing with flesh the bare fragmentary bones that survive in the archæological record and for revivifying the human societies that have created it. It was by reference to the stone hatchets, still used by the newly discovered Amerinds, that Mercati in the sixteenth century correctly interpreted the stone celts (axe- or adze-blades) that had hitherto been treated as natural phenomena—namely thunderbolts; only three hundred years later did the recovery of celts still mounted as axes in their wooden handles from the Swiss lake-dwellings provide direct archæological evidence for their use. Since then archæologists are constantly finding equally convincing and illuminating explanations for otherwise incomprehensible relics and monuments in the equipment and technology of savage or barbarian tribes still living in South America, New Guinea or Borneo.

Not only does the equipment of these modern savages and barbarians who know neither bronze nor iron, still less aluminium and uranium, illustrate the use of formally similar objects or structures uncovered in Europe and the Near East. A study of their mode of life reveals how communities with an equally limited and defective equipment can in fact cope with environments comparable to those that must once have confronted our own prehistoric ancestors and forerunners; it shows how men can actually wring a subsistence out of a very uncompromising environment with a minimum of material equipment, however laborious and precarious the adaption to that environment may have been. We could not imagine with any sort of realistic detail how the mammoth-hunters of South Russia survived the Ice Age nor how Neolithic peasants gained a footing among the virgin forests of Central Europe without the living paradigms offered by the Esquimaux and the Papuans.

For accurate parallels to the older documents of European prehistory, archæologists have generally to look to Australia or Africa. But in the remoter unindustrialized corners of Scotland, Norway or the Balkans are yet to be found small communities still practising crafts known to have been plied by their prehistoric ancestors and employing implements—e.g. fish-spears and fish-weels—of precisely the same form as those lost in peat-mosses seven thousand years ago. In Great Britain Cecil Curwen[1] and, following him, Grahame Clark[2] have made brilliant use of the data offered by European folklore to explain both the function and also the functioning of many a prehistoric European artifact. In the functional classification of an European relic or monument an analogy from Europe itself is of course preferable to one drawn from Africa or the Pacific. In the first case not only is the environment more like the prehistoric. There is a real likelihood that a continuous tradition links the prehistoric to the recent artifact. The wicker fish-traps recovered

[1] For example in *Antiquity*, XII, 1938, 261–89.
[2] *Prehistoric Europe; the Economic Basis*, Cambridge, 1954.

from Danish sites of the Maglemosean culture are identical in form with those still used by Scandinavian and Finnish fishermen, they are also made of the same material and by the same technique and used in the same way. It is absurd to assume that this very ingenious and quite improbable device has been re-invented *n* times in seventy-five hundred years. Evidently Scandinavian fishermen of today are efficient heirs of a tradition that goes back unbroken, despite all intervening changes in climate, technology and population, to the Mesolithic Age!

Thus for interpreting archæological relics from northern Europe analogies in the contemporary folk-culture of that area are more useful and more reliable than any parallels, even though they seem more exact, from Tierra del Fuego or British Columbia. Similarly in interpreting the housing and equipment of the early Sumerians of southern Iraq, the marsh Arabs of that region are likely to be more helpful than West African Negroes or Malays. In fact in Hither Asia, Iran, the Indus valley and along the Nile traditional modes of behaviour seem to have persisted from the Bronze Age and before more completely and obstinately than in even the remotest corners of Europe. Beer for instance is still brewed in Egypt by processes prescribed in hieroglyphic and cuneiform texts and inferable from earlier archæological data.

In the absence of any hint of such continuity of tradition ethnographic clues to the function of an archæological datum are always somewhat suspect and may prove deceptive. So-called tracked stones (pebbles with narrow grooves on a flat face) resemble exactly pebbles used by Amerinds for sharpening bone pins and awls; they were accordingly classified as pin-sharpeners when first collected in Scotland. Subsequently a complete series was recognized that illustrated every stage in the development of such almost unshaped pebbles to well-fashioned specimens that are found with bronze mountings accompanied by tinder-boxes and iron strikers in Scandinavian graves. The latter are unmistakably strike-a-lights—fire-producing implements—and the ruder and older tracked stones of Scotland must be thus classified. Closer examination has in fact disclosed the presence of iron rust in the grooves of some examples. Ethnographic parallels in fact afford only clues in what direction to look for an explanation in the archæological record itself. Mercati's genial interpretation of the stone celts from Europe was after all only universally accepted after the discovery of mounted specimens in the Swiss lake-dwellings.

If material culture be defined to include all reasonably efficient means for the attainment of attainable social ends, we must include among the latter desires and purposes that *Homo sapiens* does not share with any other animal. In the case of weapons of war this difficulty does not arise; for some animals are provided with corporeal weapons used and adapted for intra-specific rather than, or as well as, interspecific hostilities. For instance stags use their antlers chiefly for fighting other stags during the rutting season rather than for defending themselves against, say, wolves. On the other hand no other species of animal evinces a desire for intoxicants such as has become a socially recognized need among nearly all known human societies. The same is true of the tobacco-smoking and betel-chewing already discussed. Such aspects of material culture result from distinctively human needs.

Such too would seem the modern desire for rapid travel recognized by 'western' societies that have provided social instruments for its satisfaction in railways, automobiles and aeroplanes.

The last-named 'need' has been entertained and approved by only a small fraction of the human species and is being 'diffused' before our eyes in the wake of means of satisfying it. The same may well have been true of the older artificial needs, e.g. for intoxicants, that are now virtually universal. Yet express trains and motor-cars that provide modern transport are the direct descendants of wagons and sledges one or another of which has been in use for six or ten thousand years and may still be found among almost every human group. If a need for rapid transport be not only distinctively human but peculiar to a small section of humanity, it is only an exaggerated form of a much older and more nearly universal human need. The means for its satisfaction can also be documented from the ethnographic as well as from the archæological record.

Now sledges and carts can be made almost entirely of perishable materials. So, apart from a very few exceptional finds from bogs or deserts, they are known to archæologists only by fragments of metal fittings or by representations that are nearly always ambiguous, and in all cases essential structural details remain obscure. These can be recovered, if at all, only by an appeal to modern analogies. In their tripartite disk wheels and chassis frames the carts of the prehistoric Indus civilization agree exactly with the village carts used in the Indus valley today. On the analogy of these latter the missing pole, yoke and body can confidently be restored on the prehistoric models. But though the tripartite disk wheel is a most improbable device that must have been diffused from a single centre, the foregoing analogy cannot be extended to other regions like Mesopotamia or South Russia where tripartite disk wheels are attested in the third millennium. On the contrary a model recently discovered from the Kalmuk Steppes shows that there the tripartite disks supported a vehicle quite unlike the Indus village cart, but much more like the *arba* of Upper Eurasia.

Once more then the equipment employed today by savage, barbarian or at least non-industrialized communities for the satisfaction of even peculiarly human needs, documents for archæologists the sort of devices that may have been used by early historic or prehistoric societies. It cannot legitimately be invoked to illustrate details of the precise device any such early society did actually use. When more than one different modern analogy can be found for an incomplete ancient relic or monument, that drawn from the same region or ecological province is likely to give the most reliable hints for the reconstruction of the latter for reasons already indicated on page 48.

If with the above reservations folklore and ethnography can be used to supplement archæological data in the reconstruction of the material culture of past societies, can they help us to recover the 'spiritual culture' of the latter and to define the function of the puzzling phenomena provisionally classified as 'ritual'. The founders of scientific archæology certainly entertained high hopes that they could. Archæology joined the ranks of the sciences when, and indeed just because, 'natural selection' and 'the survival of the fittest' had won general acceptance for the Theory of Evolution.

Archæologists and anthropologists or ethnographers were evolutionists too. While prehistorians, like de Mortillet (page 25), were arranging archæological data to illustrate an unilinear evolution of material culture, anthropologists like L. H. Morgan[1] in America and Tylor[2] in England were arranging the data of comparative ethnography to document an equally unilinear evolution of human culture as a whole—of social organization, religious institutions as well as technology. All human societies, they imagined, had progressed along parallel lines through the same evolutionary stages towards a single goal, represented by nineteenth-century capitalist democracy, but at different rates. Ethnography disclosed societies whose progress had been arrested at some stage through which American and British societies had also passed but in prehistoric times. If then many articles of equipment used by the contemporary Esquimaux could be exactly matched from Magdalenian settlements in France, Esquimaux and Magdalenians were in the same technological stage; indeed the Esquimaux were living representatives of the late Pleistocene reindeer-hunters of Europe whose evolution had stopped short at the point reached in France during the Ice Age and who had not participated in the advances subsequently made in more temperate climes. Accordingly their behaviour could be used not only to fill up the gaps in the archæological account of Magdalenian material culture (e.g. to reclothe the Magdalenians in fur suits), but also to interpret the symbolism of their spiritual culture, the conventional meaning of which had been forgotten in Europe for fifteen thousand years.

[1] *Ancient Society*, New York, 1871.
[2] *Primitive Culture*, Oxford, 1871.

The invocation of ethnographic data for the functional classification of archæological phenomena was encouraged by the Materialist Concept of History, formulated by Karl Marx[1] also in the fateful year 1859. He argued quite convincingly that means of production and relations of production are interdependent in the sense that a technology can only function within an appropriate economy or system for distributing the product and that the relations of production in turn determine in the long run the ideological superstructure—codes of morality and law, superstitions and religious beliefs, artistic expression and so on. Briefly this is equivalent to saying that what we have called material culture determines spiritual culture. Many Marxists, even in Russia before 1950, confused 'determines' with 'causes'. In that case it would follow that if the material culture of a prehistoric community was the same as that of a contemporary barbarian tribe, its spiritual culture must also be the same and these barbarians' rituals and beliefs could be confidently attributed to their Neolithic European counterparts. In fact of course the determination by technology Marx postulated was anything but mechanical causation. If a certain kind of religious belief facilitates the operation of a given technology and therefore be likely to accompany it, its concrete expression in symbolic acts, the results of which alone survive in the archæological record, enjoys great latitude and cannot be inferred with any confidence from the technology. Nor is it really practicable to establish an identity between the technology of any contemporary tribe with that of any prehistoric community.

In general there is no sort of evidence that human

[1] *A Contribution to the Critique of Political Economy.*

culture has advanced everywhere along parallel lines.[1] There is no guarantee that a society, like the Australian Aborigines, having once devised a material equipment adequate to maintain it in an unchanging environment, thereupon stopped imagining new means for achieving those unattainable ends that all human societies seem to approve. Indeed there is evidence that rituals and their material symbols have changed. Finally, not even technological progress is necessarily unilinear. No doubt as the aims of technology are attainable, the efficiency of any instrument for the attainment of such an end is mathematically determinable; the efficiency of a tree-felling device for example is inversely proportional to the number of man-hours consumed in felling a tree with its aid. That does not mean that a steel saw, driven by a petrol motor, is absolutely more efficient than a stone axe. Only by virtue of a highly improbable conjuncture of circumstances is the social labour time consumed in extracting and processing the metal and fuel, in fashioning the saw and the engine and transporting the products so nearly equal to that required for converting a local pebble into an axe-head that the greater rapidity of the imported machine gives it a real advantage over the home-made tool!

A radically different method of filling the gaps in the archæological record from ethnographic data has been suggested by the 'Culture-historical School' of Roman Catholic missionaries headed by the late Father W. Schmidt. These claim to be able by comparative methods to disentangle from the allegedly composite cultures of savage and barbarian tribes living today in the New World, Oceania and Africa a limited number

[1] For a fuller discussion, see my *Social Evolution*, London, 1951.

of primary 'culture cycles' that once existed independently and can be detected pure in the archæological record.[1] Their claim implies a theory of culture as a mechanical aggregate of 'culture traits' that sociologists unanimously condemn as unscientific. Their selection of constituent 'traits' from the ethnographic record often seems arbitrary, as if dictated rather by the theory than objective relationships between them, while some of their alleged archæological counterparts turn out to be imaginary, like Neolithic 'pile-dwellings' in Switzerland.

In fact no existing society today is so exactly the representative of any past society, known exclusively from archæological data, that its rituals or social institutions can provide precise and reliable explanations of the more puzzling relics and monuments recovered from the prehistoric past. A study of the superstitions, institutions and equipment of the simpler peoples of today reveals the endless diversity of human behaviour and can suggest uses to which otherwise inexplicable archæological data may have been put. Azilian painted pebbles are rather like some Australian churingas, so quite possibly they may have served as magical repositories of souls, but they are just as likely to have symbolized something quite different. The patterns on other churingas agrees almost exactly with certain West European rock-carvings, but they are known to mean toads and gum trees, a plant unknown in Europe. The long houses built in Europe by Danubian I and First Northern farmers resemble in plan so closely the long houses of the North American Iroquois and the Kayan of Borneo respectively that it is tempting

[1] Menghin, *Weltgeschichte der Steinzeit,* summarized the ethnographer's conclusions and tried to apply them to prehistory in 1931.

to infer that they were inhabited by the same sort of enlarged family or clan. But that is just an alluring inference that at least theoretically might receive confirmation by future observations for instance on the disposition of furniture and equipment in the houses and on the arrangement of fields round them.

Nor is the assistance proffered by psychoanalysis more substantial. Rites and their fossilized results and instruments may well be symbolic expressions of suppressed wishes of the Unconscious (itself by the way a mythological entity). The interpretation of dreams, however, reveals the unimaginable diversity of symbols thus employed by the Unconscious. Their meaning can be elucidated only by the slow analysis of a whole series. It is hardly likely that one would hit upon the precise meaning of one symbol, fossilized and isolated from its contents.

In fact the superstitions and unattainable aspirations of prehistoric societies are in detail unknowable. Does that matter? We can at least guess at their general character. What is more important, objective data justify inferences as to the influence of 'spiritual culture' on other aspects of behaviour. We can estimate the economic role of the temple or the tomb in the concentration of wealth and accumulation of a social surplus without knowing in any detail what rites were celebrated therein or still less what beliefs and hopes these symbolized.

CHAPTER FIVE

When was it made?

If you ask an archæologist the age of a building or an implement he will answer 'Tudor', 'Akkadian', 'Micoquian', 'Cortaillod', 'Reinecke BI', 'Childe's Scottish III' or something equally illuminating. In the first two cases he may perhaps concede so much to your ignorance as to add, 'That is, late sixteenth century A.D.' or 'early twenty-third century B.C.' But in so doing he is relying not on archæological conclusions, but on the statements of literary historians or assyriologists. He might similarly condescend to explain 'Micoquian' as equivalent to 'late last interglacial', but in so doing he speaks as a geologist and no longer as an archæologist. If still further pressed, he might hesitantly murmur, 'Well, say about 110,000 years ago', but to do so he has abandoned geology as well as archæology and relies upon astronomy. To the remainder no archæologist would attach any figures without a cautionary explanation, at least as long as the present chapter!

These outlandish names and mystic figures are really just conventional labels for seriated divisions of the archæological record, for sections of archæological time. Archæological time exhibits seriation but not duration. The record can be divided up into a series of consecutive culture-periods and sub-periods. Or rather, we should say, the records can thus be divided into a number of such series; for each series has only local validity. These series of periods provide a chronological frame in which archæological events, the results of human actions, can be arranged. But the periods themselves are constituted precisely of such results. An archæological period is just that period of time during which a particular set of types were current in a certain province, in other words during which the human population of that province continued to behave in a manner that left particular marks on the archæological record. The first business of archæological chronology is to establish sequences of such periods, what may be called the culture sequence for each province. Any such a sequence provides the basis for a *relative* chronology; in it the position of any one period, relative to all the rest, is determined, but not its duration nor its position in the series of sidereal years reckoned from the Christian, or any other arbitrary, era nor even its relation to the sequences established in other provinces. If it were possible to correlate exactly the several sequences recognized in all provinces, archæologists might claim to have established their own *absolute* chronology. But the local sequences must first be settled.

The local sequences have been built up primarily on a method borrowed from geologists; the foundation of all archæological chronology is *stratigraphy*. In sedimentary rocks, laid down under the sea or on the floor of a lake, the first sediments to be laid down will be at the bottom of the deposit unless subsequent movements of the earth's crust have upset the order. In general terms, 'in any undisturbed deposit the oldest layers are to be expected at the bottom, the latest on the top'. This formulation applies to archæological deposits too.

Caves have been repeatedly frequented by groups of men; during each occupation broken implements, discarded ornaments, bones left over from repasts, ashes and other refuse will be dropped and trodden into the cave floor, forming a habitation layer or culture-stratum (French *foyer*). If the cave be then deserted, cave-earth falls from the roof, or stalagmite may form a sterile layer. The latter will seal the underlying habitation layer, but may form a floor on which men, eventually returning, will deposit a second occupation layer. A repetition of this cycle yields a stratified series of occupation deposits, each later than the one below it. Plainly the artifacts and other data in each deposit constitute an assemblage of associated types in the sense explained on page 32. And the assemblages, or at least some of their constituent types, from the several layers will normally differ one from another. The geologists who first examined the Palæolithic deposits in French and Belgian caves singled out as 'type-fossils' those types that varied from layer to layer. They found that assemblages, characterized by the same type-fossils, succeeded one another in the same order in a number of caves in France and Belgium. In other words they found that such assemblages were always *homotaxial*. They went on to infer that such assemblages were contemporary—in archæological time of course—and used their type-fossils to define archæological periods or culture periods. Any assemblage in which Moustierian points and side-scrapers or Magdalenian harpoons and batons occurred was accordingly assignable to the 'Moustierian' or to the 'Magdalenian period'.

This concept of type-fossils, like the idea of stratigraphy, was of course taken over directly from geology. In that science it was found that certain genera or species of fossil plant, fish or mammal were distinctive of a particular bed of sedimentary rock and that beds containing them were everywhere homotaxial, i.e. in every stratified series of beds the layer containing them occupied the same position in relation to strata bearing different type-fossils. Once a fossil species has thus been found distinctive of, and peculiar to, an homotaxial stratum in the record of the rocks, it may be taken as a type-fossil of a geological period. Any rock containing that fossil, even when found unstratified, is assigned to the period thus defined. In just the same way did Moustierian points and side-scrapers define a Moustierian period for archæologists.

It must at once be admitted that this application of the geological concept of type-fossils to archæology has proved unsatisfactory for reasons some of which have already been indicated (page 27) while others will appear in the sequel. Similarly the geological principle of superposition, devised for dealing with strata a hundred or more feet thick, may be reliable when applied to cave deposits, separated by impermeable sterile layers, but demands extreme caution when applied to other archæological deposits. In the later archæological periods the filling of a disused ditch or of a rubbish pit constitutes a well-stratified deposit. In general the layers of rubbish thrown into it will form a series with the earliest material at the bottom and the latest on the surface. But the activities of men, rodents and earthworms may disturb the sequence and transfer individual artifacts from the layer in which they had originally been deposited to a higher or lower level.

For Neolithic and later periods the commonest and most useful stratigraphical sequences are provided by settlement sites, continuously occupied for many generations. Such often assume the form of low mounds, technically termed *tells*—an Arabic word meaning 'mound' or 'hill'. In South-eastern Europe and South-west Asia villages generally have consisted of agglomerations of houses built of pounded earth (*pisé*) or mud-brick. Such houses will not stand up for ever; after fifty or perhaps two hundred years water will sap the foundations and the whole structure will collapse like a mud pie. No irregular heap of angular debris is thus left to be cleared away; the walls have gone back to mud and can be stamped flat to serve as the floor of a new house on the same spot but at a slightly higher level. In the meantime the narrow lanes may have become so choked with refuse thrown into them that the street level is flush with the new house floor. By a repetition of this process over several centuries the site of the village has grown into a lofty mound with the latest hamlet on its summit.

A tell thus formed offers an ideal stratigraphical sequence. The houses at each level, together with the relics left lying on their floors, and—please note—those found in pits and drains dug down from those floors and accompanying corpses interred beneath them—constitute assemblages of associated and archæologically contemporary types. Type-fossils recognized therein, if found in homotaxial deposits in other stratified tells, are well suited to characterize an archæological period. Now there are two ways of excavating such a tell to recover from it a stratigraphically certified culture-sequence.

Often a test pit is sunk through the superimposed strata composing the mound. The level—i.e. the depth below or the height above some arbitrary datum—is registered on each relic recovered and all relics collected within the same 10 or 50 cm. are kept together. The total content of collections from successive levels will probably be found to differ statistically; that is, while a few sherds of pottery of style B occur from bottom to top the bulk of it is concentrated in level — 3 (levels are generally numbered from the top downwards, the inverse of the order of deposition and should then be, but seldom are, prefixed by a minus sign); similarly style A pottery, represented by relatively few sherds in level — 3 absolutely predominates in level — 5 while level — 2 is characterized by a preponderance of style C ware that is scarce in — 3 and still rarer in — 5. These observations suffice to establish a sequence of ceramic styles from our tell. If the same sequence be observed at one or two other sites, pottery styles A, B and C may be taken as type-fossils for three consecutive archæological periods. Period A is just the interval of time during which style A pottery was fashionable and so on.

The collections derived from such arbitrary levels cannot rank as associated assemblages. In test-pits it is scarcely possible to recognize disturbances, so that relics lying at the bottom of a silo dug down from a house in layer — 2 and belonging to that period may be included in the collection from layer — 5. Small relics from the first occupation will be lying about the site and may well be included in the mud used for building all later houses. Similarly scraps from high levels may slide down the sides of the pit or down the burrows of animals or insects into lower levels. Such excavations can disclose a sequence only of such types as are represented by many hundreds of examples. They cannot be relied upon for fixing the stratigraphical position, the relative age and the chorological co-ordinate of rare individual objects. As a result the cultures, whose sequence has been determined only by test-pits, are liable to be represented exclusively by a few type-fossils, and all too often prehistorians speak of a 'culture' when they mean only a ceramic style. But of course once the chronological position of a ceramic style has been stratigraphically determined, the content of the culture it symbolizes may be enriched, for instance, by the furniture of graves containing the distinctive pottery but also other articles. Graves, however, are not always available.

The above defects can be obviated by employing the far more expensive and time-consuming method of removing a complete tell, or a substantial area in it, layer by layer. In this case the 'levels' are defined, not by measurement from an arbitrary datum but by actual floors. (These are generally recognizable by 'feel', but in any case should be definable by wall-foundations and hearths.) The contents of pits and graves dug down from such floor levels, together with the relics trodden into, or lying on, the floors proper and the monuments themselves constitute associated assemblages, the whole contents of which are archæologically contemporary.

The assemblages thus recovered from each successive floor level do not necessarily differ sufficiently to define distinct archæological periods. Such are usually defined by easily recognizable differences in type-fossils. Consecutive layers, not thus distinguished, are generally assigned to one and the same period. So the excavators of the tell of Tószeg in Hungary[1] distinguished no less than twenty-three floor-levels, but could recognize only three archæological periods.

A statistical study of the total assemblages from each level would doubtless allow of a finer periodization. But there are limits to such refinement (cf. page 81). Not all changes in fashion nor all fluctuations in the fortunes of a single community can profitably be used to define the boundaries of fresh periods. Notoriously today fashions in skirts change faster than fashions in trousers, while revolvers have been more rapidly improved than knitting needles. Neither male costume nor male armament alone would provide reliable type-fossils; these should reflect changes in many aspects of social behaviour affecting a plurality of distinct communities dispersed over a substantial area. Stratigraphical excavation of the Heuneburg,[2] an Iron Age fort on the Upper Danube, revealed six consecutive occupations interrupted by dramatic historical events —the destruction of the fortifications by hostile attack and their rebuilding, each time on a new principle. Yet Heuneburg II to V were all assigned to the same archæological period, Hallstatt II (HD Reinecke); for all four alike yielded type-fossils (brooches, vases), recognized as defining that period, which recur in many graves and forts between the Rhone and the Odra. (In 1954 the period has been subdivided as prehistorians have learned to distinguish two assemblages of type-fossils over most of that area, so that

[1] Mozsolic, 'Ausgrabung in Toszeg 1948', *Acta Archæologica Hungarica*, II, 1952, pp. 25 ff.

[2] *Germania*, 32, 1954, pp. 25–56.

Heuneburg II–III will now be assigned to Hallstatt IIA, IV–V to IIB.) Historical events affecting only a single community do not initiate new periods, archæological or historical, but only such as effect whole regions, like the Norman conquest of England.

All too often no stratified settlement sites are available to establish a culture-sequence. Throughout temperate Europe, for instance, sites were seldom continuously occupied or repeatedly re-occupied in prehistoric times. Even when they were, the dwellings were seldom so closely packed together that successive buildings were directly superimposed while the decay of their wattle-and-daub walls did not build up layers of deposit into tells. In many periods no settlement sites at all are known; the Middle Bronze Age of Britain, Denmark and South-west Germany, for instance, is represented in the archæological record solely by graves and hoards. In default of stratigraphical evidence different assemblages of types, recurring associated together in a single region, can with due precautions be arranged in temporal sequences by comparative typological methods.

The differences between two such assemblages recovered from the same site or province may be due either to changes in fashion and technical improvement with time or to the divergent traditions of contemporary, but historically distinct, societies. Now in a single cemetery the second alternative can generally be dismissed as unlikely. So recurrent differences in grave goods are probably chronological. In a cemetery of two hundred or more well-furnished graves it should be possible to divide the graves and their furniture of types into at least three groups on the following principle: each group should be characterized by its own distinctive assemblage of types, but some of the distinctive types, normally found in group I graves, occasionally occur in group II graves, associated with group II types, and *vice versa*; similarly group II types are sometimes found in group III graves and *vice versa*, but group I and group III types are never associated together in the same grave. If these conditions be satisfied, the three groups represent as many temporally distinct and consecutive periods.

This method of establishing chronological sequences is obliged to proceed by *tripartition*, not by any Hegelian metaphysic or trinitarian mysticism, but by the very nature of the material to be seriated. And of course by the same process any one of the three periods can in turn be subdivided into three provided the graves are numerous enough, and sufficiently richly furnished and the fashions reflected in the grave-goods and burial rites sufficiently plastic. With several cemeteries each containing a thousand or so well-furnished graves Petrie[1] on similar principles, though differently formulated, worked out the famous system of fifty 'Sequence Dates' (S.D. 30–80) for the division of Egyptian prehistory, but for practical purposes this yielded only three 'periods' styled originally Early, Middle and Late pre-dynastic, but later rechristened Amratian, Gerzean and Semainian. Subsequently the validity of this sequence was stratigraphically demonstrated while two earlier 'periods' were prefixed to it.

But whereas in Neolithic Europe owing to the shifting nature of the rural economy there are no continuously occupied and therefore stratified village sites, large cemeteries regularly used for burials over several generations will be equally lacking. In the furniture

[1] 'Sequences in Prehistoric Remains', *J. Anthrop. Inst.*, XXIX, 1899.

collected from small groups of graves scattered over a wider area, it is almost impossible to distinguish local from chronological differences—differences due to the divergence of traditions from those due to changes in one and the same tradition. When, however, owing to active and regular commerce manufactured articles were imported and used by many different societies, these 'international' types are generally quite conspicuous, and naturally differences between them must almost inevitably be chronological. In the Bronze Age the British Isles, Northern Europe and Central Europe, including the Middle Danube basin and Upper and Central Italy, engaged in a really astonishingly frequent interchange of metal gear and of course other commodities. In most regions hoards and well-furnished graves offer varied assemblages of metal weapons, tools, ornaments, toilet articles, vessels and so on. In these local types can easily be identified by their concentration in a limited area when their distribution is plotted on a map (page 116). Not too seldom there is found associated with these in a grave or hoard a foreign type—i.e. a type shown by the above criterion to be proper to another locality while some types—notably vessels of beaten bronze—are so 'international' that they may turn up associated indifferently with almost any appropriate assemblage of local types.

Obviously differences between international types, fulfilling the same function, are likely to be only chronological. Thus Velatice, Jenšovice and Hostomice cups, all obviously identical in function and yet all evenly distributed from Jutland to the Carpathians, must owe the small variations that distinguish them to changes in fashion in the course of time. At the same time application of the rule of tripartition enunciated above, to the assemblages from a single natural province yields a division of the local bronze age into three or more typological periods. In Denmark, southern Sweden and North Germany, Montelius[1] distinguished six such periods numbered I to VI and today generally cited as Montelius I, II, etc. (abbreviated MI . . .). In the different assemblages from south-west Germany and Bohemia, Reinecke[2] subsequently distinguished also six periods, but labelled them Bronze Age A, B, C and D, and Hallstatt A and B (abbreviated (B)A, B, C, D and HA, HB); for the last two labels Childe and Hawkes[3] propose to substitute the letters E and F respectively. Several of Montelius' and Reinecke's periods are now in course of subdivision and there are good prospects that a nine-fold division will emerge for both areas. In Britain reliable closed finds are so relatively scarce, that agreement has been reached only on three (or at best six) periods.

Thanks to the frequent interchange of commodities between the regions mentioned the several local series can to some extent be correlated, and a tripartite division of the European Bronze Age into Early, Middle and Late has already received fairly general approval. It must, however, be insisted that this scheme is applicable only to the regions traversed by the main arteries of the European metal trade. No Middle Bronze Age is recognizable typologically in South France or Spain; the 'Bronze Age' of South Russia and

[1] 'Om Tidesbestämning inom Bronsealder' (K. Vet. Hist. o. Antikvitets Akademien), *Handlingar*, Stockholm, 1885.

[2] His system has never been clearly set forth, but the main outlines are indicated in several papers in *Die Altertumer unserer heidnischen Vorzeit*, ed. Lindenschmidt, vol. V, Mainz, 1.

[3] *P.P.S.*, XIV, 1948, pp. 176–218.

the Mediterranean basin lies outside the European scheme. When applied to the Ægean or Palestine terms like 'Early' and 'Middle Bronze Age' denote, not only a totally different assemblage of types, but almost certainly an equally different slice of historical time. In the Balkans no Bronze Age in either the European or the Ægean sense has yet been recognized by types of metal gear.

Tripartition or some cognate principle yields reliable sequences of consecutive periods, but in itself does not indicate their direction, i.e. which period is the first or the last. The direction of the sequence must be determined by stratigraphy or other independent criterion. When Petrie first divided a predynastic cemetery into a series of consecutive grave-groups, he actually inverted the sequence, making it begin with an assemblage subsequently shown to lie at the end of the series. In a cemetery, though superposition is excluded, what has been called 'horizontal stratigraphy' may provide a serviceable alternative. It is theoretically likely that the community's earliest graves have been dug as close as possible to a patriarch's tomb, to the local shrine or church or to some other 'hallowed spot'. Successive generations thereafter will have to be content with locations ever farther away from the imagined focus of life-giving magic. Hence assemblages of grave-goods, collected from ever-widening zones, should represent ever later generations. This method has been applied with promising results to a couple of urnfields in south-west Germany, but awaits elaboration and refinement through practice.

In default of stratigraphy the aid of *typology* in its strict and primary sense must be invoked. It assumes that some of the constituent type-fossils change step by step, but always in one direction, and that this direction can be determined by inspection. The idea, like many others, was borrowed from natural sciences —evolutionary biology and palæontology. Tools and machines, like organisms, have evolved by progressive modifications towards increasingly efficient forms, the triumph of which is secured by 'natural selection'. Last century the founders of scientific archæology watched this process repeatedly being illustrated before their eyes in the rapid evolution of ploughs, fire-arms, railways and ships, while the author and many readers have witnessed even more dramatic serial and cumulative advances in aeroplanes and wireless apparatus. The process is conveniently presented visually by the locomotives, automobiles, and flying machines arranged, in chronological order, in any technological museum or by pictures of such in albums. It yields what is termed a typological series; provided you know the relative positions of any two types in the series, you can arrange all the rest in the right chronological order without looking at the dates obligingly stamped by manufacturers on their engines.

Prehistoric artifacts, like axes, stabbing weapons, razors and safety-pins, though they bear no date of manufacture, can be arranged in series of the same sort, and on the same conditions the terms of such series can be used as type-fossils to distinguish successive periods in archæological time. Devolutionary series can also be constructed, just as legitimately. A classic instance, provided by Celtic coins, was traced by John Evans[1] as early as 1849. The barbarian Celts first used Macedonian coins. Then, when they began

[1] 'The evolution of Ancient British Coins from Philippi', *J. R. Numismatic Soc.*, 1849.

to mint their own, they at first copied the Philippic with the king's head and inscription on one face and the Sun in his chariot on the other. To the illiterate barbarians these symbols were meaningless and were reproduced by each generation of moneyers less and less intelligently until they became mere curvilinear patterns such as Celtic artists love, though deprived of all recognizable representational content. A similar gradual degeneration of pottery copies of metal buckets or situlæ can be seen. These were repeatedly reproduced long after the metal originals had gone out of fashion or become unobtainable locally. The later copies diverge increasingly from the model and come to lose all distinctively metallic features. The metal original could indeed hardly be deduced from the latest products, but familiarity with the intermediate stages leaves no doubt as to the continuity of form throughout the whole series.

Typological series played a leading role in the construction of schemes of archæological chronology. Thomsen's Three Ages were after all typological stages. De Mortillet's divisions of the Old Stone Age were purely typological in this sense. Montelius' divisions of the Northern Bronze Age were based in the first instance on evolutionary series of daggers and swords, axes, razors and brooches. Since his day arm-chair archæologists in their studies have been busily engaged in arranging pots, instruments and ornaments of many kinds, or pictures of these and plans of tombs and houses to illustrate logical evolutionary or devolutionary series. They have even used their results as a frame for quite comprehensive schemes of relative chronology. Yet typology is a rather dangerous device and must be used only with due precautions.

In the first place the direction of a series can hardly ever really be determined by inspection. Even the 'efficiency' of a tool or weapon is not discoverable *a priori*. As in organic evolution 'the fittest' are just those that do 'survive', so with prehistoric implements. The socketed celt of bronze did in fact eventually replace all other types of axe-head—not only the flat axes,

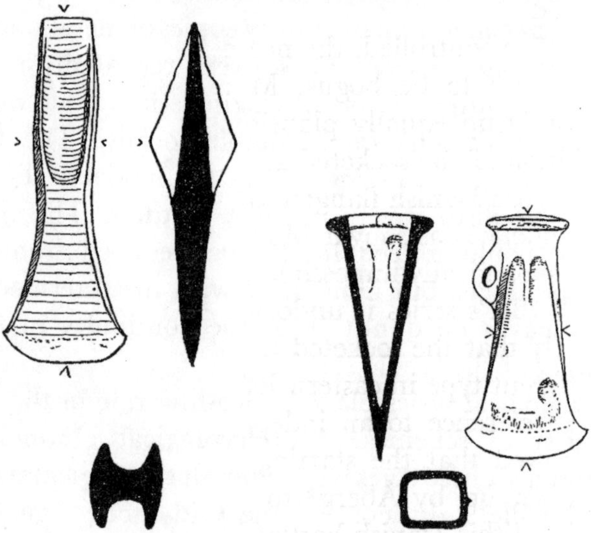

Palstave and Socketed Axe.

winged axes and palstavs from which it was supposedly evolved, but also the shaft-hole axe that in a cheaper medium, iron, ousted the socketed celt itself. In bronze the latter proved its superior efficiency by surviving, but this superiority could scarcely have been deduced *a priori* without the knowledge of its historical demonstration. Even with that knowledge no one explained how the socketed bronze axe could have been more efficient than a one with a shaft-hole through the head since the latter type in iron has proved itself the most efficient till I noticed in 1953[1] that a socketed axe head contains only half as much bronze, and therefore costs half as much, as any other form with the same width of blade. The direction of a so-called evolutionary or devolutionary series actually needs to be controlled by some independent criterion like stratigraphy, just as much as the sequences discussed on page 69.

When thus controlled, the neatest typological series may turn out to be bogus. Montelius and Sophus Müller drew up equally plausible series to illustrate the evolution of the socketed axe from Italian winged axes and from Danish flanged axes respectively. Contextual evidence has shown Montelius' logical scheme to be chronologically impossible while the most crucial step in Müller's series is undocumented. It is indeed quite likely that the socketed axe developed out of a quite different type in eastern Russia or Central Asia. Similarly reference to an independent chronological frame showed that the starting point of a plausible series drawn up by Åberg[2] to explain the origin of Middle Neolithic Danish battle-axes must be far later than any of the axes supposedly derived from it!

Secondly the several functional classes of artifacts have progressed at different rates, just as some orders and phyla of living organisms have evolved faster than others. Certain fossil molluscs or insects reappear in almost every geological stratum from the Palæozoic to the present day while quite new phyla, genera and even species have been emerging and evolving. So too in successive layers of a tell weapons types may change

[1] 'The Socketed Celt in Eurasia', *Xth Annual Report*, University of London, Institute of Archæology, 1954.

[2] *Das nordische Kulturgebiet in Mitteleuropa*, Stockholm, 1918.

progressively while querns—hand-mills for grinding grain—may persist unchanged from the lowest to the topmost level. The concept of type-fossils in archæology, as in geology, expressly makes allowance for differential rates of change. Those types are selected by preference that have been found to change conspicuously from strata to strata. In using typological series for the chronological division of the archæological record, prehistorians should never rely on a single series alone. The several stages of one series, say of daggers and swords, can normally be correlated by association in graves and hoards with corresponding stages in other series, for instance, axes and brooches. The accepted typological divisions of the Bronze Age, as already indicated, rely upon two or more parallel series, the several stages in each of which can be correlated by association. Phenomena representing the same stage in an evolutionary series should be called *systadial*. Those occupying the same relative positions in parallel typological or stratigraphical sequences may be termed *homotaxial*.

Now in geological time homotaxial types are considered to be also synchronous or contemporary. All rocks everywhere that yield fossil *ceratites* are assigned to one and the same geological period, the Triassic. The evolution of species and genera yields a chronological frame of reference, adequate to contain the events that interest natural historians. The frame provided by the evolution of artifacts is too coarse for an adequate appreciation of the events of human history. Human societies notoriously progress at different rates and differential rates of change are among the more significant phenomena of history. They would be simply obliterated by using a chronological frame in which Maori culture of the eighteenth century A.D. was contemporary with North European culture of the eighteenth century B.C. because the stone axes of each were systadial.

Again each new species in the geological record presumably emerged first at one focus—or at most a very few—and spread thence slowly all over the globe. The use of that species as a type-fossil excludes the possibility of identifying this centre. The changes in archæological type-fossils that have been used to distinguish archæological periods are each the expression of a new idea that arose in the brain of an individual. Archæology has renounced the attempt to identify the individual inventor or innovator (page 8), but may legitimately hope to recognize the society that approved, adopted and realized the invention. The interval between the adoption of an invention by this society and its diffusion by one means or another should therefore be relevant to human prehistory. Now the type-fossils selected by archæologists to define periods in a sequence are all too often just those used to define cultures—that is the societies themselves.

For neither purpose do archæologists use devices that have indeed certainly been diffused, but that once adopted have survived for a long time owing to their high efficiency under particular conditions or owing to some other circumstance. While the flintlock marks a well-defined stage in the evolution of firearms, its survival in Africa in the twentieth century would make it an unreliable dating fossil while its adoption by many societies that have preserved their cultural independence excludes its use for defining cultures. The same arguments apply to tripartite disk wheels or saddle querns. The first use of such evolving types could be profitably used to mark a chronological horizon only among societies and in regions which were in close and continuous intercommunication such as would be attested *inter alia* by participation in subsequent advances.

Under the so-far unique conditions of the twentieth century the construction of railways, motor roads and landing strips might be taken to mark consecutive stages that were not only systadial and homotaxial but archæologically synchronous almost all over the Globe. Several of the types used for the subdivision of the European Bronze Age (page 67) were of this kind since some specimens were conveyed by trade from the cultural province in which they were normally manufactured to regions where quite distinct local types were current. But these type-fossils provide valid chronological guidance only within a single commercial system. Greater circumspection is demanded in using types locally manufactured or transported only in the course of folk-migration.

The European Iron Age, like the Bronze Age, has been divided up by typological criteria, and the first subdivision of the First Iron Age or Hallstatt period is conveniently distinguished by a long cavalry sword, most commonly found in graves where it is often accompanied by an appropriate scabbard and horse-trappings. So distinctive is it that Hallstatt I is often described as the 'period of the long Hallstatt sword' since in Hallstatt II a short sword replaces the longer weapon. Graves thus furnished are concentrated round the head-waters of the Labe, the Danube and the Rhine; they are rare west of the Saone and Rhone and there are only a couple beyond the Garonne. It looks as if these graves in South-western France belonged to immigrants, and, if so, they may be quite substantially later than those in the immigrants' homeland round the slopes of the Alps. Other items of furniture or ritual in fact prompt the suspicion that they may really be Hallstatt II despite the long swords!

Again the very distinctive style of hand-made pottery, termed Halafian, being made in a large number of villages in Assyria and in North Syria between the Tigris and Euphrates and in all at the same relative level immediately before the al Ubaid style came into fashion, has quite rightly been taken as the type-fossil for a division of Mesopotamian prehistory. Can the same pottery—i.e. vases of the same form, made and painted in the same way and with identical patterns—be taken to mark the same period when it is being made much farther west in the Orontes valley or on the Mediterranean coast? Unless this particular ceramic art had been introduced by itinerant professional potters, in which case Halafian pottery could not be used to define a culture, it must have been carried by migrating groups of farmers whose migration might have occupied quite a number of generations.

As a third warning example, since de Mortillet, bifacially worked flint spear-heads (laurel leaves) have been accepted as type-fossils to define both a Solutrean period and a Solutrean culture. In Belgium and France these type-fossils do normally turn up in homotaxial layers, but not so in Spain; for at Parpallo the Solutrean is immediately followed not by a Magdalenian culture as in France, but by a 'Solutro-Gravettian' more like the Gravettian, that precedes Solutrean in France and Spain, than the Magdalenian (cf. page 26). In South Russia the position is even worse since the nearest approximations to Solutrean types lie below, not above, the eastern counterpart of the Gravettian. In a word, divisions of the archæological record distinguished by locally made types can be extended beyond regions where the types homotaxy is stratigraphically attested only at the risk of confusing the chronological with the chorological classification. Only types manufactured at a single focal area and distributed thence by trade or war, whether they be Irish decorated axes, black-figured Attic vases or German fly-bombs of V I type, provide unimpeachable synchronisms between distinct sequences; every ruin layer in western Europe and every camp in the aggressor country where bits of these fly-bombs are found will correctly be treated as contemporary by future archæologists.

To some of our American colleagues the traditional Old World practice of defining cultures by a few type-fossils and of 'dating' an assemblage by the presence of one or two such type-fossils must seem terribly crude and unscientific. Instead of relying on differences in two or three types to distinguish one horizon or culture from another, should we not rather look for statistical differences in the composition of total assemblages? After all, we admitted on page 34 that an archæological culture or period is to some extent a statistical concept. In fact archæologists are confronted with assemblages that ought to be chronologically or chorologically distinguishable but which yet comprise just the same range of types. In the early post-glacial period of Northern Europe for instance, assemblages, derived from consecutive pollen zones and therefore differing in age, seem all to contain precisely the same stone types. It turns out, however, that the frequencies of the several types in stratigraphically consecutive assemblages do differ significantly while assemblages collected from the same pollen zone agree reasonably well.[1] In such cases we simply must rely on statistical methods.

But such are applicable only under certain rather unusual conditions. We need assemblages each comprising ten to forty distinguishable types and not less than five hundred classifiable specimens. Then we can calculate the percentage of each type represented in each assemblage, express the result graphically in a frequency diagram—a histogram or a cumulative graph—and compare the results.[2] Given an adequate sample, such a frequency diagram no doubt defines an assemblage much more reliably than the presence of one or two flake-axes or geometric microliths. Of course the statistical methods impose on the archæologist a much more comprehensive and exhaustive collection and examination of data than was usual in the nineteenth century; it is not sufficient to preserve and record only a limited range of recognized types, still less only nice museum pieces. Every fragment must be scrupulously preserved, classified and counted if a 'random sample' suitable for statistical analysis is to be obtained. They require of the investigator a lot of admittedly simple, but still laborious, calculations to which he may be unaccustomed. But these burdens should be welcomed.

There remain graver theoretical and practical obstacles. Statistics are designed for the treatment of

[1] C. A. Althin, 'Man and his Environment', *Arsberattelse*, K. Hum. Vet. Samfundets i Lund, VI, 1954, 275 ff.

[2] The best practical illustrations of the statistical method are to be found in Bordes studies on the French palæolithic in *L'Anthropologie*, 1950 and 1951.

numerically large samples; laboriously to calculate the frequencies of daggers, swords, spears, axes and so on in graves that normally contain at most ten grave goods would not even produce an illusion of precision. In practice only collections of stone work or pottery from domestic sites are likely to offer an adequate number of specimens, so that the range of application for statistics in archæology is drastically limited. Even within these limits the significance of a specimen may be quite disproportionate to its numerical representation in an assemblage. Querns are never likely to bulk large in the collection from any site. Yet one quern, representing perhaps 0·2 per cent of the stonework from a site, would on current definitions suffice to transfer the whole assemblage from the Mesolithic (or Miolothic) to the Neolithic bracket!

The differences between two assemblages are not necessarily due either to chronological or chorological factors. The debris from a flint mine will inevitably present a different composition from the collection made on a farm-house site. The winter-quarters of the North European Maglemoseans, if ever located, will surely yield a statistically very different assemblage of relics from that recovered from their temporary summer camps that are all we know at present. Indeed from the frequency diagrams we would hardly believe that both assemblages represented the seasonal behaviour of one and the same people. But on both sites one might hope to find the same type-fossils albeit in quite disparate proportions. Before chronological or chorological conclusions can be drawn from a statistical comparison between two assemblages great care must be taken to discount other distorting factors.

Nor is the subjective element entirely eliminated.

What the statistician counts and averages are not units, differing merely in metrical characters, but types, and as we have insisted, an arbitrary element must enter into the discrimination of types. If statistical analyses are to be conducted co-operatively by several independent workers, the unit types must be very narrowly defined. The total number of types will then become embarrassingly large. Alternatively, using somewhat broader definitions, there would arise so many borderline cases on which no two classifiers need agree, that each might draw a discrepant frequency diagram from the same assemblage! In practice, if a major cultural phase, say the Upper Palæolithic of France, is to be subdivided by the composition of consecutive assemblages rather than by the presence or absence of a few type-fossils, it will be necessary to re-examine all well-stratified and comprehensive assemblages, re-sort them on a very precisely defined typological system and perhaps revise the current divisions on the new basis. This laborious procedure may make it possible to assign to a precise horizon assemblages of flints vaguely termed, for instance, Magdalenian, though the absence of the accepted type-fossils of bone and antler precludes a definite diagnosis.

In cases like this where accepted type-fossils are not preserved, or like the Tószeg tell where the range of types remain constant through several building periods (page 64), statistical methods are likely to make possible a finer and more reliable chronological division or periodization. But the results will still have a very limited application. They may justify us in synchronizing two occupation sites, appropriate layers in two caves or two tells. They are useless for assigning a relative date to a grave or to an unexcavated site. On the other hand the discovery of a single well-established type-fossil in a grave or on the surface of a mound, at once dates relatively the whole burial or one occupation of the mound. Hence statistical methods are not likely to replace the older typological ones, however valuable they may be as supplements thereto.

The relative age of any closed find, the position of its contents in the local culture sequence, must be that of the latest type-fossil or type-fossils it contains. Now a grave or hoard may contain type-fossils of differing relative ages. A hoard of florins, buried today, might comprise coins of all English sovereigns from Victoria to Elizabeth II. The latest type alone gives the date of the burial or the deposition of the hoard. Obviously our florins could not have been buried before the reign of Elizabeth II. On the contrary it is the oldest type associated with it that gives a relative date for the foundation of a building, used or occupied over several periods. For example the erection of a collective tomb must have been completed before the first interment was laid to rest in it and must be assigned to the period represented by the oldest dateable types found in the tomb; for these presumably are the surviving remains of the furniture accompanying that first burial. Similarly the excavation of the fosse defending a fort or castle must be dated by the oldest relics recovered from it.

Of course the first rule does not mean that all the contents of a closed find must be as late as the latest item. Plainly from our hoard of florins no one would infer that Queens Victoria and Elizabeth II were contemporaries nor even that Victorian florins were being minted in 1954. But just that sort of false inference can easily be drawn from the grave-groups or hoards on which the typological division of the record by tripartition depends. For we have admitted on page 66 that 'group I types are sometimes associated with group II types'. Now on our rule such graves must be assigned to period II, and *ex hypothesi* none of the types in them are independently dated as are our florins. Of course the answer is that the remaining types are much more frequently found associated together and with other group I types uncontaminated by any group II admixture. But when the total number of closed finds is small—a hundred or so—this answer may not sound convincing. In this case some mathematical procedure should be devisable to measure the validity of our answer. Appropriate formulæ have yet to be invented and are likely to be rather complicated and certainly laborious in application.

CHAPTER SIX

How Long Ago did that Happen?

BY stratigraphy, by some sort of typology or by a combination of both methods it has been possible to establish serial divisions of the archæological record in a large number of more or less well-defined archæological provinces. All are divisions of archæological time though, owing to the nature of that time, its divisions are of quite indefinite length or duration. The divisions are therefore generally, though not very happily, termed 'periods' or more accurately 'culture-periods'. However, when the differences distinguishing consecutive divisions consist merely or mainly of modifications of types in form, style or technique without any radical or comprehensive break in the general continuity of tradition, these divisions are often, but unfortunately not always, described as 'phases' or 'subperiods' in a period.

On the analogy of the familiar divisions of the geological record a certain number of such consecutive units may be grouped together as constituents of larger divisions, traditionally termed 'ages'. But of course these ages have no more precise duration than the periods that compose them. Though everywhere homotaxial, the boundaries of the ages need not be, and are not in fact, everywhere synchronous. Of course the major divisions used in Prehistory are Thomsen's Three Ages with the modifications described on page 25 and distinguished by the material used for the major cutting tools and weapons.

The Three Age system has indeed provided an indispensable scaffolding without which a finer and more logical division could never have been constructed. Yet it admittedly suffers from grave defects. Perhaps the most serious objection to the current use of the Three Ages is that they seem to be invested with the same global sense as the corresponding major divisions of the geological record. Not even the major divisions of archæological time can be usefully given the same absolute value as geological eras and epochs, as Mesozoic, Cenozoic, Eocene or Pleistocene. Units of time suitable for measuring major processes of Natural History are too large for the faster tempo of human history. Stone, bronze and iron, used for cutting tools and weapons, are technological stages, and the technological changes used as criteria did in fact react to a varying extent on other aspects of material and spiritual culture. The Three Ages are everywhere demonstrably homotaxial. It does not, however, follow that all societies assigned to any one of them were systadial in an—imaginary—process of unilineal social evolution. Still less were such societies everywhere contemporary. It might be wiser to replace the word 'Age' by 'Stage'. If it be considered too late to effect this reform, it will be necessary as a rule to qualify the 'age' with a geographical adjective. 'Burial in oak-tree coffins was characteristic of the earlier part of the Bronze Age' would be a false statement in a book on the social history of humanity or even on European prehistory, but quite legitimate in a chapter explicitly headed 'Northern Europe'; otherwise the adjective 'North European' must be inserted before 'Bronze Age'.

The subdivision of the first Stage or Age gives ground for more valid complaints. Prehistorians admit today not three but five Ages, and to distinguish Palæolithic, Mesolithic and Neolithic have introduced new bases of division, substituting palæontological and economic criteria for the technological one used by Thomsen to define the three original divisions. For defining equivalent divisions of the whole archæological record, the criteria adopted for distinguishing Palæolithic, Mesolithic and Neolithic are indefensible.

But for a subdivision of one of the ages or stages thus defined, a new basis of division may quite logically be introduced. Even so, for defining substages, the criteria used to distinguish Palæolithic, Mesolithic and Neolithic are illogical, and new divisions, more consistently defined, simply must be substituted.

If Palæolithic be defined by the same criteria as, and therefore be coterminous with, a geological epoch, the Pleistocene, it becomes superfluous as a division of archæological time. Technologically and from the point of view of general cultural content, the contrast between Lower and Middle Palæolithic on the one hand and Upper Palæolithic and Mesolithic on the other is enormously greater than that between Palæolithic and Mesolithic. This contrast at least should be given terminological recognition on lines proposed by Rellini and elaborated by Menghin.[1] Lower and Middle Palæolithic should thus be grouped together as Protolithic or Archæolithic and contrasted with a Mio-

[1] Menghin, *Weltgeschichte der Steinzeit.*

lithic (or as Breuil suggests, Leptolithic) embracing what are now called Upper Palæolithic and Mesolithic. These two substages would remain everywhere homotaxial and could be distinguished by easily recognizable criteria such as the use of bone, antler and ivory.

The proposed reform of terminology would at least reduce the difficulties involved in applying the current English criterion for delimiting the last division of the Stone Age. The beginning of food-production—the cultivation of plants and/or the breeding of animals for food—was unquestionably a more significant change in the life of the societies affected, and influenced all aspects of culture more profoundly, than the adoption of grinding or polishing as a means for edging axe-blades; the latter technological criterion is thus a less suitable basis for defining a new substage than the radical innovation in the primary economy, the food-quest. In practice the criterion is not so readily applicable; from a few bones it is not easy to distinguish domesticated from wild animals; actual remains of vegetable foods are only in exceptional circumstances preserved. Hence all evidence for farming might be missing unless the farmers made specialized and easily recognizable implements for reaping or grinding grain—and there are no reasons for suspecting that the very earliest farmers did.

Prehistorians once hoped to dodge this practical difficulty, believing that all farmers manufactured pots and most at least polished stone for axe-blades. Since 1950, however, it has been demonstrated that the earliest farmers in Palestine, Cyprus, Kurdistan and Baluchistan did not make pots, while at least in Palestine they made no recognizable axes at all and certainly made none with polished edges. Pot-making is thus not necessarily connected with food-production and cannot be invoked as a reliable indicator of the latter. Conversely plenty of communities are known, particularly in the coniferous zone of northern Eurasia, that made quite good pottery and a whole carpenter's kit of polished stone, but certainly cultivated no food-plants and seem to have kept no domestic animals save dogs. These societies undoubtedly lived at a time when Neolithic farmers were already clearing the deciduous forests immediately to the south. In so far as 'Neolithic' denoted a period of global time, they were therefore 'Neolithic' and the use of this term could be justified further by assuming that they had learned pot-making from these not too distant Neolithic farmers. (Recent observations both in Denmark and the Sudan point to the local manufacture of pottery before Neolithic farmers can be detected in either area!) Such a use of Neolithic is, however, both illogical and misleading. It could be avoided by terming food-gatherers, surviving after the rise and spread of food-production, opsimiolithic. Such food-gatherers of course survive to the present day; it would be ridiculous to call the Australian Aborigines or the Bushmen of the Kalahari either Palæolithic, Mesolithic, or Neolithic as long as these terms denote at once bits of sidereal time and technological stages; Miolithic, confined to the latter meaning, would appropriately designate both.

In 1950 Pittioni[1] of Vienna suggested another solution, by creating an Age (or Stage) distinguished by the first use of a new, durable material—pottery. The Lithic Age (*Lithikum*—comprising the old Palæolithic

[1] 'Historischer Ablauf und urgeschichtliche Terminologie', *Anzeiger d. phil.-hist. Kl. d. Österreich. Ökad. d. Wissens.*, 1950, No. 5, pp. 57–70.

and Mesolithic) would on his scheme be succeeded by a Ceramic Age (*Keramikum*) that would last until the discovery and use of a further industrial material initiated the Metallic Age (*Metallikum*). This system is quite logical and would accommodate comfortably the hunter-fishers of the Eurasian taiga without reducing them to the same stage as the Australians who would of course be classified in the Lithic Age (Stage). The objection to it is quite other; the invention of pottery did not in itself usher in anything like so far-reaching changes in human life as the adoption of food-production or even the use of metal for tools and weapons. So I should prefer to keep my old Stone (or, if you like, Lithic) Stage, but subdivide it into a Palæolithic, Miolithic and Neolithic. I do not for a moment expect that archæologists in general will accept either logical scheme.

The Bronze Stage is less likely to cause confusion, but its name at least is open to criticism. In the first place it is chemically incorrect. Unalloyed copper can be distinguished from the alloy, bronze, with certainty only by analysis, spectrographic or quantitative. Analyses have now shown that the vast majority, and in some cases all, the metal objects from the Early 'Bronze Age' of Palestine, Egypt, Anatolia, South Russia and several other provinces were made of unalloyed copper, while in several regions the alloy was never regularly used at all even for 'Late Bronze Age' types like socketed celts! It would be more correct and logical to replace 'Bronze' by 'Palæometallic'.

The chemists' objection cannot be removed by inserting a 'Copper Age' or a 'Chalcolithic Stage' or both between the Stone and Bronze Ages (Stages). That expedient is in the first place impracticable since copper and bronze are often superficially indistinguishable while there are no prospects of having enough metal objects analysed to constitute a reliable sample. Secondly, while unalloyed copper was presumably used before the advantages of a tin-copper alloy were discovered, the employment of bronze did not in fact universally replace unalloyed copper. On the one hand in some areas, as for instance in Northern Europe and China, knowledge of metallurgy was probably introduced from elsewhere by craftsmen who had already learned the superiority of bronze so that locally a true 'Bronze Age' appears without a preliminary stage in which unalloyed copper alone was employed. On the other hand, owing to the relative rarity of tin, some communities, e.g. in Anatolia and South Russia, failed to secure supplies of that element sufficiently regularly to allow of the general industrial use of bronze until both copper and bronze had been supplanted as material for tools by iron. In other words the use of unalloyed copper does not mark an universal homotaxial stage in technological progress.

Finally the superiority of bronze over unalloyed copper is far from being such that its adoption marks a technological advance of such far-reaching consequences that it marks a significant phase in cultural development. As to Chalcolithic, the term's use is due to a misapprehension of the whole basis of classification. If it means anything, it must mean a phase during which stone tools were still used side by side with metal ones. Of course there are everywhere assemblages containing both metal and stone tools, often metal and stone axe-heads even. Indeed, save in specially favoured regions, copper and still more bronze were so costly that arrow-heads and tools for rough work were often, and sometimes always, made of stone throughout the whole 'Bronze Stage'. By the original definition of the Age, any type ever associated with a metal tool or weapon was to be assigned to the 'Bronze Age'. This should mean that any assemblage or culture in which recognizable local metal types occur, however rarely, is to be classified in the Bronze Stage. Occasional imported metal objects, evidently the products of a metallurgical industry in another province, do not justify the attribution of the local assemblages in which they occur to a local Bronze Age. Thus stray Irish halberds or Bohemian pins, imported into Denmark or South Sweden, do not make the graves in which they occur 'Bronze Age'. Local imitations, though closely copying the foreign models, would mark the beginning of the North European Bronze Age.

Once the foregoing principles are grasped, there is no practical difficulty in distinguishing a local Bronze or Palæometallic Stage. It is only a failure to appreciate the criteria agreed upon that led such authors as Weibull to deny the existence of a Bronze Age in Denmark and Scandinavia on the ground that, despite the wealth of metal gear in graves, domestic sites yielded no metal relics, but a considerable range of stone tools. Professors Hawkes and Piggott recently startled British prehistorians by dramatically announcing 'Beakers are Neolithic'. All these authorities have just misunderstood what archæologists are classifying and labelling. The chronological labels under consideration were never meant to be attached to slices of clock-time. They are applicable only to assemblages of archæological phenomena repeatedly associated together. They denote simply the position of such assemblages in a local sequence and their relation to other assemblages in the same sequence.

If this be so, do the Three Ages, even subjected to the reforms just proposed, now serve any useful purpose? The materials used for cutting tools and weapons provided an *a priori* sequence with the aid of which prehistoric assemblages could be arranged serially at a time when no other evidence for seriation was available. Now that stratigraphy has provided plenty of more objective and concrete sequences, Daniel[1] has suggested, the old divisions and their labels have become superfluous and even misleading. No doubt if in any region it were certain that the whole range of the culture-sequence was fully known, the Ages and their subdivisions could profitably be replaced by the series of natural numbers. But many parts even of Eurasia are so imperfectly explored archæologically, that only disconnected members of the local sequences have so far been identified. These can be 'chronologically' classified only by Thomsen's criteria. Even in the best explored regions of Europe prehistorians have been repeatedly startled by the unexpected discovery of quite novel assemblages. Thus within the last ten years new Neolithic cultures or facies have been identified in regions so intensively studied as England, Denmark and Thessaly. Here again something has been gained by labelling them 'Neolithic', even though their precise place in the local sequence is still unsettled.

After all the requisites for a good classification are that its criteria should be precise, easily applicable and informative, i.e. such that, if you know to which class a phenomenon belongs, you should be able to deduce

[1] *The Three Ages*, Cambridge, 1941.

certain significant characters of it. The Three Ages satisfy more or less even the third requirement. The label Bronze Age, for example, indicates not only the approximate position of a culture in a sequence but also suggests a good deal about its technical potentialities—not only the mastery of metallurgy, but also the possibility of making things demanding metal tools such as wheels—something of its economy—at least trade—and even of its sociology, the existence of full-time specialists. Of course this technological, economic and sociological information is obtained at the cost of a loss of precision as to the classified culture's chronological relation to other cultures, even closely adjacent cultures. For that a different framework is required. Till such be available, the Three Ages provide a useful scaffolding.

But its limitations and provisional character must never be forgotten. There is no sense in saying that the industry of a Central Australian tribe is Aluminium Age, while apart from a few patently imported pen-knives and kerosene tins the home-made equipment is manufactured entirely of wood, bone and stone. So it is meaningless to call the Rinyo culture (represented for instance at Skara Brae in Orkney) Bronze Age just because similar pottery may be associated with Beaker pottery that in turn is sometimes associated with bronze articles. It is equally absurd to call Beakers 'Neolithic' because bronze is found in less than 5 per cent. of the known Beaker graves. Just as a coin hoard is dated (i.e. the date of its deposition is limited) by the latest coin comprised in it, so a culture or assemblage of associated types must be given the archæological age of the latest type ever associated with it. Since bronze is in fact found in some graves of the

Beaker culture, the whole culture is archæologically dated by them, but as no genuine Rinyo assemblage ever contains any bronze nor even objects fashioned with metal tools, that culture can remain Neolithic.

Of course two communities on quite different technological levels do live and have lived side by side. The types proper to each alone determine their assignment to one or another Technological Stage or Archæological Age and by definition will assign them to different Ages. Their actual contemporaneity can be demonstrated only by appealing to different criteria—i.e. to alien types, appearing sporadically as imports in assemblages of both cultures or as imported by one from the other. Such criteria serve to synchronize (i.e. to establish synchronisms between) stratigraphical or typological divisions of distinct culture-sequences—divisions that are components, rather than subdivisions, of the 'Ages' and need not therefore always be assigned to the same 'Age'.

These divisions of local culture-sequences, termed culture-periods, like the more comprehensive 'Ages', have to be distinguished by conventional labels. Three distinct systems of period nomenclature are in fact in use today. (1) A period may be treated as a subdivision of an Age and designated by the Age name qualified by an adjective such as Early, Middle, Late, Lower, Upper and so on. This system is used to distinguish periods within the Bronze Ages of Palestine and of Temperate Europe. It has recently been applied by Danish and Swedish prehistorians to designate periods of the local Neolithic. Strictly speaking a geographical adjective—Palestinian, British, Danish—is needed in addition to the temporal or stratigraphical qualification. Even so it can legitimately be objected that culture-periods are not in fact subdivisions of technological Stages and that to pretend they are may lead to confusions of the kind just indicated. The practice is quite deplorable when the 'age name' denotes an imaginary or unnecessary 'Age' like the 'Chalcolithic'. Spanish prehistory was for a long time divided into *eneolitico inicial*, *pleno*, and *final*, and one can only hail with relief the abandonment of this terminology by our Spanish colleagues. Even worse is the use of these pseudo-ages as periods without qualification. Deplorably the culture-sequence in Turkey was divided by von der Osten into 'Chalcolithic', 'Copper' and 'Early Bronze' Ages, and unhappily his nomenclature is still current. (2) De Mortillet borrowed from geology the practice of naming periods after sites where the type-fossils were first identified or are well represented. Generally adopted for the Old Stone Age, this system of nomenclature has subsequently been applied to divisions of the culture-sequence in Egypt, Mesopotamia, Siberia and elsewhere. Now the type-fossils used for the distinction of culture-periods which were in fact originally regarded as stages of Culture (in an holistic sense), are generally the same as those used for distinguishing cultures (in the partitive sense). Hence naming a period after an eponymous site, is equivalent to giving it the name of a culture.

The practice of applying one and the same name to a period and to a culture has been responsible for horrible confusion and remains an obstacle to clear thinking. Some evil results of attributing a global significance to divisions of the culture sequence observed in France have been indicated on page 27, but by no means all. The terms Aurignacian, Solutrean and Magdalenian denoted cultures that succeeded one another in that order in parts of France. Each was distinguished by a definite assemblage of easily recognized types and to call a lance-head Magdalenian not only suggested its relative position in a sequence, but also defined its form and the archæological phenomena with which it was likely to be associated. But no Magdalenian types occur in Russia, and so to call any artifact from Russia Magdalenian is only a way of saying that it belongs to the last archæologically distinguished phase of the Pleistocene. The boundaries of cultures are in fact spatial, as well as temporal, and the denotation of their conventional names must be equally limited.

This fact is slowly being accepted. But then the chronological use of the culture-name involves a needless multiplication of period names. In southern Mesopotamia the terms Ubaid, Uruk and Jemdet Nasr denote cultures, that succeed one another, and are accordingly used to designate successive periods. The Ubaid culture is found in northern Mesopotamia too, so the southern culture names were at first applied to the two succeeding divisions of the archæological record—wrongly since their contents on the whole are quite distinct from those of the homotaxial divisions in the south. To eliminate this confusion the terms Ninivite and Gawra have been introduced to denote the last two periods in the northern sequence. An historian is thus obliged to learn two sets of conventional names—needlessly since in this case the northern cultures are not only homotaxial, but also roughly synchronous with the southern.

On the other hand two cultures even in a small area are often partially contemporary. So in parts of France the Solutrean overlaps with the late 'Aurignacian' (i.e., Gravettian) in others, while in south-eastern Spain it is not even homotaxial with the French Solutrean. These overlaps and unconformities are inexpressible in a terminology by which Solutrean denotes a division of archæological time.

The name 'Hallstatt' again illustrates the ambiguities arising from such a terminology. Originally used to designate the assemblage of Early Iron Age types represented in the cemetery of salt-miners at the eponymous site, it was soon extended to cover all assemblages north of the Alps belonging to the First Iron Age, even though the most distinctive types familiar at Hallstatt were unrepresented therein. P. Reinecke further applied it to certain 'Late Bronze Age' assemblages that never contained iron tools or weapons in the—largely erroneous—belief that they did comprise types of beaten bronze ware represented at Hallstatt. On the other hand the epithet is also applied to a more restricted series of graves and their contents that are characterized by a very distinctive armament. No one encountering the word 'Hallstatt' in an article can tell whether the author means the first division of the Iron Age, the final Bronze Age, or a specific culture within Iron Age I!

(3) Some of the foregoing confusions are avoided by a third system of nomenclature, analogous to that applied to the 'Ages': periods are designated after type-fossils distinctive of stages in the development of one culture. So in Denmark and southern Sweden each of the three recognized Neolithic periods used to be named after the form of megalithic tomb fashionable in it alone, even though within the period some communities, i.e. cultures, did not build megalithic tombs at all. This procedure gave the series Dolmen, Passage

Grave and Stone Cist periods—in Swedish *dös-*, *gånggrifts-*, and *hällkist-tiden*. In Greece the terms Geometric, Orientalizing, etc., are similarly used. The system has at least the advantage of honesty. 'Passage Grave period in Denmark and Sweden' means just the period during which some communities there were building and burying in passage graves and can be applied to all types represented in passage graves or demonstrably contemporary with them. The geographical qualification, however, is always necessary; there are 'passage graves' and 'long cists' in Ireland, but it is unproven and indeed unlikely that they were contemporary or even homotaxial with their Danish homonyms.

Moreover the chronological indicator cannot be omitted without causing ambiguity. 'A passage grave axe' might mean either 'an axe of a type likely to be found in any grave of the passage grave period' or 'an axe of a type peculiar to passage graves and their builders'. Hence to make an adjective out of the period name on this system an English-speaker at least would have to resort to the cumbersome periphrasis 'of the X period in Y province' (e.g. 'an axe characteristic of the Passage Grave period in northern Europe'). Finally 'passage graves' and 'the geometric style in art' are themselves type-fossils distinctive of cultures as well as of phases in the development of culture. They denote chorological as well as chronological co-ordinates. And so after all do the chronologically qualified 'Age names', in so far as these are descriptive. Both systems are therefore open, albeit in lesser degrees, to the same objections, as have been raised against the use of culture-names.

In fact what archæologists have to classify chronologically and arrange in sequences are not isolated data—relics and monuments—but the recurrently associated assemblages of such that we have termed cultures. What the chronological classification has to exhibit is the relations between cultures in archæological time. Conventional designations of a qualitative kind do serve to exhibit the seriation of assemblages, and as long as the number of assemblages to be seriated remained unknown and the only recognizable relations were actually serial, descriptive or site names offered the most convenient available labels. But the use of culture-names or even a disguised form of such to denote divisions of archæological time, automatically excludes the recognition of the cultures, thus designated or described, as existing side by side within such divisions. As soon as overlaps or synchronisms between cultures can be detected by archæological means, the systems of nomenclature considered above have become both confusing and redundant. Names preempted for chorological groups or descriptive of typological stages can be replaced by labels indicative solely of position in a series—i.e. by natural numbers.

In every well-explored province the serial divisions of the archæological record should, as Daniel has contended, be distinguished by numbers that indicate order but not duration, like Petrie's 'Sequence Dates' (page 66). Each division will still be distinguished from the preceding one only by some change in culture. It will in fact be constituted by one or more cultures, but at the same time will contain these. Of course numerical designations can only be applied in practice where the culture sequence is so far known that the total number of culture-periods, likely to be distinguishable, can be roughly estimated. For the archæologically almost virgin soil of Central Asia Further India or even the Balkans, cultures will stil constitute irreducible divisions of archæological time to which their names will have to be applied.

But even in the well-explored provinces of the British Isles, northern Europe and Greece, recent surprises have warned us that familiar and well-recognized culture-sequences may be susceptible of extension and subdivision. Allowance for such refinement can be made by using Roman numerals for the major periods already recognized. Divisions in each could then be denoted by letters and subdivisions by Arabic figures; so we might have III B I (or even III B I c, using a lower-case letter for further subdivisions!). It will surely be found essential to number separately divisions of the Pleistocene and of the Holocene (i.e. of the old Palæolithic and of the Mesolithic with subsequent 'Ages'). There would also be advantages—and disadvantages—in numbering separately subdivisions of the subsequent 'Ages'. Clark has familiarized British readers with Mesolithic I, II and III for Northern Europe and these might logically be followed by 'North European Neolithic I, II and III'. On the other hand the Ertebølle culture, characterizing Mesolithic III, is very largely contemporary with the Tragtbaegre culture of Neolithic I. Both could live comfortably side by side in North European III z or IV x, but not in Mesolithic III y or in Neolithic I u!

In any case each numbered series must be qualified by a geographical adjective. On the one hand in some provinces changes in culture are more frequently reflected in the archæological record than in others so that the number of practicable divisions is larger. On the other hand divisions in any one province are based upon a locally-established culture-sequence and can only exceptionally be synchronized with divisions similarly based in another province (cf. page 102). At present we can only hope to be able to talk of British III B or North European VI A 2.

Even with these limitations the conversion of our numbered divisions from a series of archæological events into a frame within which those events happen encounters unexpected difficulties. Suppose we define an archæological province as a more or less continuous area throughout which two or more cultures occur and are proved to be everywhere homotaxial. The British Isles would then certainly rank as a single archæological province. Now in 1940 I was able to divide the culture-sequence in southern England between the beginning of the Neolithic Stage and the Roman Conquest into nine reasonably clear periods. In Scotland I could distinguish only five, in Ireland not more than four! What system of numeration can be applied to the whole province? Does the failure to distinguish in Ireland any good counterparts to the cultures that occupy periods VI, VII, VIII and IX in southern England mean that the Irish record covers a shorter interval of time than the English, i.e. that the Neolithic Age began later in the former country? Were the Overhanging Rim Urns, characterizing Irish period III (it could be called IV by 1950), really synchronous, as well as homotaxial, with the similar urns of English V? The last question, that of synchronizing events in different parts of the same province, raises the wider problem of synchronizing the divisions of the distinct culture-sequences in different provinces.

What prehistorians demand from their chronological classification is not an array of disconnected sequences of periods each defined by events, but a comprehensive frame of reference within which events in different provinces can be compared, so that it would be possible to say that a given event, say the adoption of cremation, occurred earlier in one province than in another. Theoretically this frame can be built up by establishing synchronisms between periods in the distinct provinces. Once this has been done, say between Britain and Northern Europe, we should no longer have two periods, e.g. British III and Northern II, but a single period, perhaps North-west European II C. Ideally by extending a net of synchronisms over the whole world even the wider geographical adjective could be dropped.

Synchronisms more exact than those deducible from the spread of a culture by folk migration or the diffusion of an invention can be established only as a result of the physical transportation in the course of trade or war of suitable archæological types from one province to another. Three possible cases arise and can best be illustrated concretely from examples—unhappily for the most part imaginary—taken from the relations between the British and the North European provinces.

(1) Irish decorated axes, type-fossils for British IV, have been found as imports in graves of Northern III. If a type-fossil of Northern III, such as a flint dagger, were found in England in a grave of British IV we should have a case of *cross-dating*, guaranteeing a synchronism between British IV and Northern III (by a more roundabout way this synchronism is in fact established).

(2) An imported spear-head, distinctive of British V, has been found in a grave of Northern IV A. Hence, we can infer that British V began before or during

Northern IV A, and so we get at least a partial synchronism. If the import be a fragile object like a pot and if the ceramic type imported be known to have enjoyed only a brief vogue in the land of its manufacture, the synchronism is no longer partial, but may be treated as precise.

(3) When a locally made axe, associated with type-fossils of Northern IV, is obviously a copy of a type of British V, we can assert only that Northern IV had not ended before British V began, but we have even less evidence as to how long it may have lasted after British V began than in case (2). Both the imported British axe and the local imitation of one give *termini post quos* or upper limits in terms of the British sequence for the Northern period in which they occur. Conversely the Northern flint dagger imported into Britain would have given a *terminus ante quem* or lower limit for the appropriate Northern period. For a precise synchronism both upper and lower limits must be determined.

(4) In British II C vases of types, current already in II B, begin to be decorated with cord impressions, a device popular in Northern I B and later; accepting an undemonstrable diffusionist postulate, it might be assumed that British II C was not earlier than Northern I B. But since in Northern I C the semicircle motive, popular already in British II B, was abruptly applied to Northern pottery, a synchronism between British II C and Northern I C becomes quite plausible. Archæologists often rely on still more tenuous evidence for establishing relations between remote cultures and synchronisms between periods in distinct sequences. But conclusions, dependent upon supposed copying, are inevitably very precarious and less credible than

those drawn from the transportation of actual manufactured articles.

During the Metallic Stages interchanges of substances and even of manufactured articles that can serve as type-fossils were surprisingly frequent between adjacent regions. Instances are not altogether unknown even in the Old Stone Age; a couple of Magdalenian needles and batons, of Continental types, found in England with remains of the native Creswellian culture, may rank as 'imports' (though probably brought by bands of roving hunters rather than traders) and would establish a partial synchronism between British Creswellian and Franco-Cantabrian Magdalenian.

By cross-dating and the interchange of products archæologists might hope to build up a network of synchronisms between local periods in adjacent provinces that should eventually embrace the whole Earth. Therein all local sequences would eventually merge into a single series of global periods. The realization of this pious hope is, however, very remote. Moreover this imagined scheme might indeed be able to assign to one culture priority over others, thus locating the starting point of an invention, or a migration. It would still disclose nothing about the duration of its component periods and so could furnish no information as to the rate of cultural change and similar questions that historians might properly put to archæologists. To infuse duration into their periods, to replace culture changes—the units of archæological time—by repetitive events such as revolutions of the Earth round the Sun, in a word to establish Absolute Chronology, archæologists have generally to appeal to Philologists or Natural Scientists—geologists, botanists, astronomers or nuclear physicists.

There is just one purely archæological method whereby the duration of an archæological period might be measured in terms of years. If a village, occupied throughout a period, together with the cemetery in which the villagers were interred, were so fully excavated that the total number of households and of graves could be estimated with considerable precision, then, making reasonable assumptions as to the size of families and mortality rates, the length of the occupation and so the duration of the period could be calculated. So far the requisite conditions have never been satisfied. A few villages have been totally excavated, but in no such case has the village cemetery been discovered. A number of cemeteries have been exhaustively examined, but at most only a fraction of the settlement that provided the corpses has been exposed. For the rest, estimates based on the thickness of archæological strata are almost worthless. Calculations based on renewals of hearths, house-floors, timber posts, storage pits may under appropriate circumstances be more reliable, but can at best lead only to very approximate results, since many factors involved inevitably elude objective determination. In 1950 for their absolute chronology archæologists have to rely on 'historical', geological, botanical and nuclear methods.

(1) A small part of the archæological record covers a period of absolute time during which written historical records were being kept in parts of the world. In the literate provinces archæological periods are named after historical events and can be measured and dated by reference to the written records. In so far as the network of synchronisms, described on page 104, can be extended from the literate provinces to embrace

prehistoric periods in sequences established beyond the bounds of literacy, historic dates can be given to prehistoric periods. Surviving written records allow us to date—in terms of our era—archæological periods in Egypt from about 3000 B.C., in Mesopotamia from 2600, in Asia Minor from 1950, in China from 1300, in Greece from about 750 B.C. Though Palestine remained illiterate for another millennium, the later prehistoric periods there can be roughly dated by synchronisms with Egypt from 3000 B.C. After 1800 B.C. cross-dating provides dates, correct within a century or less, for prehistoric events in the Ægean down to 1100 B.C.

Now from 1500 B.C. Ægean manufactures began to percolate across the Alps and penetrated even to England, where they are found in graves of British IV or V. Conversely ornaments of gold and amber, of types proper to British IV, turn up in Greece during the sixteenth and fifteenth centuries and have been hailed as imports from the British Isles. If that diagnosis be correct, British IV and the corresponding periods on the Continent must have begun by 1600 B.C. (It must be admitted that the British origin of the ornaments is disputed while the date currently assigned to the undoubted Ægean beads found in Britain and Central Europe would, if correct, reduce the age of the period by two centuries.) After 600 B.C. historical dates can be extended as far afield as Malaya, by the importation of unmistakable Greek pottery, while the Roman Empire defines an archæological horizon recognizable from the Equator to the Arctic Circle, from the Atlantic to the Bay of Bengal. In the same way Chinese contacts with the outer barbarians provide historical dates for periods in provinces as far away as the Altai. There are good prospects for an extension of historical chronology to the dating of prehistoric periods over much of the Old World at least after 1000 B.C.

Attempts had been made to apply 'historic' dates to divisions of European prehistory before the synchronisms mentioned above had been discovered and to even earlier periods. On the assumption that the advances distinctive of the Neolithic and Bronze (Palæometallic) Stages originated, like literate civilization, in the Ancient East and were diffused thence, as the alphabet was, the emergence in historically dated contexts in Egypt or Mesopotamia, of Neolithic, or Bronze Age types that recur in still illiterate parts of Eurasia would give a limiting date for the prehistoric period to which they belong there. The initial assumption is of course undemonstrable and has in fact been challenged as '*le mirage orientale*'. The further assumption that any resemblance between a prehistoric and a civilized product must be due to an imitation of the latter by the illiterate barbarians is even more debatable. Even in specific cases where it is defensible on other grounds, for instance in the case of clay stamps and clay block-vases from Central Europe, the limits provided by the assumed models (that turn out to have been current for seven or more centuries) are too wide to be of much use. In any case before 3000 B.C. no historical dates are available.

For all events prior to 3000 B.C. archæologists have to invoke the aid of natural scientists.[1]

(2) During the Pleistocene in high latitudes the advances and retreats of glaciers and ice-sheets provide a

[1] Their methods have been so admirably explained by F. E. Zeuner in *Dating the Past*, London, 1951, that any full description here is superfluous.

very coarse but independent framework within which archæological events in periglacial regions can be arranged. In so far as transgressions of the sea, registered as 'raised beaches', correspond to interglacials, the same frame can be used to accommodate the littoral cultures of the rest of the Earth. And if the minima in the curve of effective solar radiation as plotted by Milankovich correspond to glaciations, absolute dates can be assigned to these geological periods. Of course, the processes involved are very gradual so that the chronological framework is extremely coarse and the 'absolute dates' can only be expressed in millennia.

(3) Throughout Northern Europe the pollen-grains, preserved in peat bogs, accurately mirror successive changes in the vegetation which serve for a division of peat deposits into *pollen zones* and for the definition of a sequence of *climatic phases*. Archæological deposits can directly be correlated with pollen zones. Of course the spread of forest trees is a rather slow process so that synchronisms between say Ireland and Sweden are far from exact and owing to local divergences of soil and climate the divisions are not identical throughout the area. This 'palinological' method can of course only be applied where extensive peat deposits are available, and its divisions are valid only within continuous regions.

(4) Pollen zones, and consequently the archæological periods correlated with them, could be given absolute dates in terms of solar years by de Geer's method of 'geochronology'. The melt-waters of a retreating glacier, discharging into a lake, normally lay down every year a double band of clay, termed a varve and conspicuously visible in a section of such

clay. By simply counting the varves in a continuous deposit, one would obtain the number of years that have elapsed since any given stage in the glaciers retreat—ideally an arbitrary 'End of the (last) Ice Age'—*Finis ætatis glacialis*. Of course no complete sequence is preserved in any single deposit, but de Geer's school claim that by fitting together partial but overlapping sequences observed in different deposits the total sequence can be reconstructed. Doubts have been expressed as to the validity of these correlations and certainly more than one varve may be laid down in a year. In any case archæological deposits or types can be related only indirectly to the varve series with the aid of the pollen zones or climatic phases provided by palinology.

(5) *Dendrochronology*. During the life of a tree a growth ring of new wood is normally formed every year and under suitable conditions the varying thicknesses of the rings form easily discernible patterns. In that case by matching early parts of the pattern on a living tree with the pattern formed in the last years of a tree used in the construction of an ancient building, it has been found possible to extend the tree-ring record far beyond the life of any single tree. At the same time the date of the felling of the ancient timber and so of the building in which it was used is given by simply counting the number of rings formed on living trees since the last ring was formed in the old beam. The method is direct and reliable, but can only be used in marginal areas where small variations in the rainfall affect tree growth markedly.

(6) All organisms absorb from the atmosphere as long as they remain alive a minute but known quantity of the unstable isotope of carbon, C_{14}, which remains

constant throughout their lives. As soon as the organism dies, however, it ceases to absorb fresh atoms of C_{14}, while the quantity already absorbed diminishes as the atoms disintegrate and turn into C_{12} at a known rate. By comparing the amount of C_{14} remaining in any piece of organic matter from an archæological deposit and deprived of life by, or for, inclusion therein with the known constant of living things, the date of the object's destruction and use by man can be precisely calculated. The system is direct and most promising, but technical difficulties and dangers of contamination at present limit the reliability of its applications.

CHAPTER SEVEN

Who did it?

THE excavator of a prehistoric site is repeatedly asked: 'Who made that?' 'Who were the people who built that house?' As an archæologist he can only reply in the same sort of terms, and often with the identical words used in answering the other stock question, 'How old is it?' He must say 'Mousterians' or 'the Rinyo folk', or something like that. To an archæologist such terms mean just as much as 'Picts' or 'Celts' or any similar name taken from a book. To a prehistorian a people are just what they did. Their culture is their behaviour, fossilized, and that is what the culture name connotes. (It is just too bad that language, popularly regarded as the behaviour pattern most distinctive of human groups, does not fossilize so that linguistic names are not applicable to prehistoric peoples.)

Similar assemblages of archæological types are found repeatedly associated together because they were made, used or performed by the same people at the same time. Different assemblages of associated types occur at the same time because they were made by different peoples. Cultures are assemblages of types that are associated because they are made by the same people. They must be classified chronologically and not themselves used to constitute divisions of archæological time. Several cultures must have existed and did exist in one and the same 'period'. One and the same culture may live through several archæological periods. For cultures are the units of the chorological, as contrasted with the chronological, classification (page 15). Having seen in the last two chapters how the chronological divisions are defined and seriated, the diagnosis, delimitation and description of the chorological divisions of the archæological record must occupy the next.

Types are found repeatedly associated together just because they result from the behaviour pattern standardized within one and the same society. This recurrent assemblage of associated types is of course a 'culture' in the archæologists' partitive sense, the unit of chorological classification. The prehistorian's business is to reconstruct the behaviour pattern that guarantees their association. Thereby this assemblage of archæological data will come to life, and the culture-name applied to it will acquire an historical connotation. A precise definition of the culture in archæological terms and an exhaustive enumeration of its contents are of course necessary preliminaries to the induction of the pattern that integrates its bits. And since so much of human behaviour fails to fossilize (page 10), only disjointed fragments of that pattern survive and may appear superficially as a random aggregate of unconnected traits. At best some traits can be seen by inspection to be organically connected; the links with the rest have to be discovered. This task is rendered harder by the nature of the traits, necessarily selected for defining a culture.

DIFFERENTIÆ OF CULTURES

To distinguish one culture from another, the most convenient differentiæ, the most serviceable diagnostic fossils are offered by the more superficial, often indeed trivial, idiosyncrasies of behaviour—traits that are least obviously integrated with the total pattern. Food-habits, for example, conditioning and being conditioned by many facets of the whole productive system are evidently more significant than table manners. Yet Englishmen and Americans have much the same taste in food, but there are subtle differences in the approved ways of conveying it to the mouth, and the latter fossilize in recognizably divergent types of implements for that purpose, i.e. of knives and forks. So an archæologist of 6666 A.D. may find himself obliged to rely on the divergences between assemblages of table utensils to help him to recognize that by 1950 U.K. and U.S.A. were not occupied by the same society!

Specialized types of knives and forks illustrate precisely the sort of type-fossils used now by archæologists to distinguish cultures of the past. For that purpose archæologists do not and cannot select the sort of equipment—automobiles, war-chariots, internal combustion engines, water-wheels—that have directly exercised the most profound influence on human behaviour just because too many quite distinct and distinguishable societies sooner or later adopt them. Such devices might indeed be well suited for dividing the archæological record into broad stages, but not for dividing contemporary assemblages chorologically. On the other hand a culture must not be distinguished and defined by one type-fossil alone. If really diagnostic of a culture it must be associated with other equally distinctive traits. Today peculiarities of knives and forks would be found associated with plenty of other fossilizing traits of the same order—spittoons or ashtrays, level or raised railway platforms . . . to help in distinguishing American from English behaviour patterns. This brings us to a second complication in the use of types to distinguish cultures.

Differences between types may be due to changes of fashion with time within the same society as well as to divergences in tradition between distinct societies. Types are in fact used to define periods of archæological time as well as to distinguish contemporary cultures. Just because a culture is to represent a society of living active men, it cannot be regarded as static; it should evolve, and the consequent changes can only be reflected in differences in its component types. Thus formal differences in knives and forks can be used not only to distinguish between English and American societies in the twentieth century, but also to distinguish English society of today from the same society in the seventeenth or sixteenth century. For English table manners have not only diverged from American, but themselves have changed in four centuries. In the present context the continuity in the latter case is just as important as the divergence in the former. This continuity in tradition should be reflected archæologically in the continuity of a typological series. It should be possible to arrange datable English cutlery in a series to exhibit locally every step in the gradual transformation of Elizabethan table utensils to their contemporary forms. It might then appear that seventeenth century English knives and forks were of the same types as twentieth century American ones or at least much more like them.

How can chronological differences be distinguished

from chorological ones? This question is constantly arising in archæological classification. In the case just cited it does not arise for two reasons: firstly the knives and forks are supposed to be independently dated; secondly the American types are concentrated in America while the English series has been collected in England. To the prehistorian the first test is not available; he is indeed often compelled to use just these typological differences as indices of age. The second criterion is, however, applicable. *Distribution* provides a criterion of the value of a type for chorological classification, for the discrimination of cultures. It also may contribute substantially to our knowledge of the content of the culture thus defined. The following discussion of the cartographic methods by which distribution is determined will accordingly take us rather beyond the immediate theme of the discrimination of cultures.

A people always inhabits a definite territory, and its extension must be in some sense orderly, though not necessarily continuous as the historical expansion of Greek colonies round the Mediterranean and of British colonies overseas should warn us as sharply as the encampments of nomads in Central Asia or North Africa. The distribution of an archæological culture should thus define the habitat of its authors, and this distribution will most conveniently be revealed by the distribution of the diagnostic types used to distinguish it. Hence if a type be really diagnostic of a culture, when its find-spots are plotted on a map, they should not appear scattered at random over an indefinite area, but should exhibit an intelligible pattern and cluster round one or more recognizable foci. Every other type, attributed on the strength of associations to the same culture, when mapped in its turn should exhibit the same general distributional pattern. If the distribution of the suspected type turn out to be really discordant with those of the remaining associated types, it loses its title to acceptance as diagnostic of that culture in the chorological classification.

Concordant distributions of type-fossils on maps will thus confirm their attribution to a particular culture as inferred from their associations in closed finds, establish their chorological value and enrich the connotation of the culture's name. Of course the distribution patterns of fixed monuments and that of movable relics are not at all likely to coincide. So in comparing distribution maps 'concordant' has a rather different meaning when applied to monuments or to relics. Portable objects like knives and forks or bulb-headed pins can easily be carried outside the territory where they are habitually made and used by traders, tourists or invaders. So some American knives and forks find their way to Britain, but, were a census taken, they would be found to form only a minute fraction of the knife-and-fork population of the United Kingdom, while the overwhelming majority of specimens hail from the United States and Canada. So in the Early Bronze Stage of Europe bulb-headed pins are densely concentrated in the Unětician provinces of Central Europe, but do appear sporadically in Scandinavia and England as a few isolated dots.

The standard distributional pattern for a relic that is a good diagnostic type will be a nucleus of thick set dots surrounded by a penumbra, or several such nuclei. Only the areas of dense concentration will represent the habitat of the culture distinguished by the plotted type. Monuments on the other hand should be restricted to the actual habitat of the culture's bearers. Roman coins turn up far beyond the Imperial frontiers in Scotland and 'Free Germany', not so Roman roads and legionary stations. In either case in comparing distributions it is primarily the clusters of find spots that are decisive; the remoter strays at least can be ignored.

When the distributions of two types are mapped and found to agree well they are said to be *concordant*. Types exhibiting concordant distributions belong to the same culture if they belong to the same archæological period. The converse of this proposition is also true. But types belonging to consecutive archæological periods and exhibiting concordant distributions are likely to belong to the same culture only if the later type is directly derived from the earlier. So Northern swords of Montelius II have much the same distribution as those of Montelius III. Even then the converse is not so likely to be true; later types are liable to have a wider distribution than earlier ones, since societies often extend the area of their habitat.

Where distributions are discrepant, no chronological or chorological inferences are permissible save in the special cases of what I term 'complementary' and 'exclusive' distributions. Both occur only between members of the same functional class—e.g. two distinct but not necessarily incompatible types of axe. The former is best explained by an example. In the Early Bronze Age of the British Isles crescentic jet necklaces frequently accompany interments associated with Food Vessels. At the same time they closely resemble, in form and details of ornament, gold lunulæ, particularly common in Ireland, but never found in any association at all. When Clark[1] plotted together on one

[1] *Man*, XXXII, 1932, No. 46.

map the distribution of jet necklaces and of lunulæ, he found the combined distribution pattern agreed beautifully with that of Food Vessels—the lunulæ filling up just those areas in the Food Vessel maps where necklaces were missing. Thus the distribution of jet necklaces and gold lunulæ can be termed *complementary*. In this case the cartographic disclosure of the complementarity of the distributions confirmed the Early Bronze Age dating of the lunulæ, for which there was no evidence from association, and their attribution to the Food Vessel culture, previously suspected on account of formal resemblances alone. At the same time it added a new trait to the Food Vessel culture. Incidentally a like enrichment of the content of a culture can often be deduced from concordant, as well as from complementary, distributions.

On the other hand types diagnostic of distinct cultures should exhibit *exclusive distributions* if they are contemporary. In the case of portable relics the interchanges effected by trading or raiding normally blur the contrast between two concentrations so that no sharp frontiers are to be expected. The distribution of monuments, if they be distinctive of two contrasted but contemporary cultures, should be more strictly exclusive and be separated by a recognizable frontier. Timber-laced forts and brochs in Scotland exhibit such an exclusive pattern. A few overlaps near the frontier in Inverness, Ross and Sutherland might reflect a rather unstable equilibrium subsisting between two opposing groups. In fact they imply that the broch culture outlasted that characterized by timber-laced forts so that its authors could plant colonies in the latter's territory. Such a survival is actually demonstrated by stratigraphical evidence and by the datable

Concordant and Complementary Distributions. After Clark.

relics found in the respective types of monument. Of course exclusive distributions do not in themselves prove synchronisms. They do help to confirm contemporancity if there be other plausible grounds for suspecting it.

Conversely types distinctive of consecutive periods, such as successive stages in an evolutionary series, rather than of contrasted cultures, should, as we said, exhibit at least partially coincident distributions. In other words, when the differences between types result from technical advances or changes in fashion within one society rather than from the divergence of traditions between distinct societies, both types would be expected to be current throughout the society's habitat. But if the people responsible expand or lose territory, these displacements will of course be reflected in the distribution maps. In Scotland, for instance, the later degeneration-types of Overhanging Rim Urn, while as evenly distributed as the earlier ones in the south, spread further northward. In southern England, on the other hand, these types are missing, their place being taken by Deverel-Rimbury Urns, the distribution of which is exclusive to that of the latest degenerations of Overhanging Rim Urns.

Cartography thus helps in deciding the diagnostic value of a type for chorological classification, in determining to which culture a type should be assigned, in establishing the contemporaneity of cultures and of the types diagnostic of them and in adding to the content of a culture phenomena never found with recognized diagnostic associations. In addition it may afford the sole means of discovering very significant aspects of a culture. The distribution of distinctive monuments and assemblages of relics, plotted on bathyorographical, geological and other appropriate maps, gives the most reliable information as to the relation of the culture they define to its physical environment. Here again the distinction between monuments indicative of settlements and portable relics must be born in mind, and not all relics are of equal value. For instance, arrowheads may mark hunting grounds rather than the sites of habitations. Still, observing proper precautions, maps can answer such questions as: 'Did the people represented by the assemblage of types select land with a view to pasture or to tillage?' 'Could they clear forest?' and so on. The location of settlements beside good fishing grounds, along natural routes of communication, or in naturally defended positions gives information as to the economy of the settlers and on prevailing political conditions.

A culture, it must be repeated, is not constituted by the few types used as diagnostic fossils, but by the whole assemblage of types and traits, associated with them within closed finds or with the aid of distribution maps and like devices. That being so, should not a culture, like an archæological period, be defined by the total composition of the assemblage rather than by the inclusion therein of two or three diagnostic types? Plausible though this suggestion may sound, the obstacles to the employment of statistical methods for the chorological division of the archæological record are graver than those against their employment for the chronological division. To the objections set forth on pages 80–2 others must now be added. Frequencies cannot be plotted on a map, types can. Significant frequencies can only be calculated from large and representative assemblages, and the latter can be obtained only from excavated sites, generally settlements.

But excavated sites of any culture are few and far between. Many prehistoric cultures are still known exclusively from graves. The majority of the data to be classified are more or less chance finds or derived from graves. But every relic of known provenance and monument recognized by superficial observation can be plotted on a map, and, once their cultural association has been determined by a single closed find, this map gives a reasonably reliable picture of the distribution of the culture that they characterize. Nothing comparable would be obtained by mapping the few excavated sites where the total composition of the assemblage has been determined. Yet without distribution maps an appreciation of those aspects of a culture just considered is excluded.

Much less than for chronological classification do all types have an equal value for chorological distinctions. For the latter purpose we want to detect divergences in behaviour patterns. Now two types of slashing sword may differ as much as a sword and a rapier and for chronological classification might both be treated as equal units. But swords and rapiers imply contrasted methods of fighting and tactics—very significant differences in behaviour—and surely should not be given the same unit value in estimating the difference between assemblages.

No doubt a quantitative element must enter into any definition of a culture. We say that a type to be diagnostic of a culture must 'normally' have been found associated with other diagnostic types. And 'normally' presumably means '*n* times'. Yet it is impracticable to fix a precise numerical value for *n*. Carved stone balls were once found in association with other types distinctive of the Rinyo culture. In the absence of any other association for these curious objects, we have to assume that the remaining hundred and twenty balls found in isolation belonged to the Rinyo culture and can be used to illustrate its one time distribution.

Of course a few stray specimens of a diagnostic type far from the region of its main concentration do not suffice to prove the spread thither of the culture they should typify. But laborious statistical calculations are hardly necessary to unmask the spurious chorological claims of such strays. No one has imagined that a baton, a needle and a harpoon turned the English Creswellian assemblage into a Magdalenian one. Again a calculation showing that, say, 18 per cent of the bronzes from Unětician assemblages in Central Europe are pins while in the contemporary Wessex graves of England pins account for barely 1 per cent of the metal ware, is an unnecessarily laborious way of stating that the Early Bronze Age peoples of Bohemia wore cloths that needed pinning while their contemporaries in Britain preferred buttoned or tailored garments!

So a culture must be distinguished by a plurality of well-defined diagnostic types that are repeatedly and exclusively associated with one another and, when plotted on a map, exhibit a recognizable distribution pattern, but it is constituted by all the types and phenomena demonstrably associated with those types. The words (1) 'plurality', (2) 'exclusively' and (3) 'well-defined' need underlining and perhaps explaining.

(1) It would normally be as wrong to characterize a culture by a single type as to constitute a culture out of assemblages in one material (page 33). Yet in some books we read of 'cultures' distinguished, if not by a

single ceramic shape or pattern, at least by pottery alone without any other equally distinctive associated traits.

(2) Ideally the diagnostic types used should be *repeatedly* associated with one another but not with types diagnostic of other cultures. They must of course be associated with non-diagnostic types or there would be nothing for them to diagnose! And unless they be *exceptionally* associated with types diagnostic of other cultures, the contemporaneity of two or more cultures could hardly be established. Even this degree of exclusiveness is often an impracticable ideal. We may have to be content with an 'unique constellation of types', i.e. with saying that only in culture *A* are types *a*, *b*, *c* and *d* repeatedly associated though type *b*, in association with types *e*, *f* and *g* may distinguish culture *B*, types *c*, *h*, *j* and *k* culture *C* and so on. Our aim should be demoting *b*, *c* and *d* from the rank of diagnostic types by finding other types *l*, *m*, *n* . . . that, being exclusively associated together and with *a*, should better define *A*.

(3) Finally, how precisely should types be defined for chorological—and for that matter for chronological—classification? No two hand-made articles are identical. All types are abstractions obtained by ignoring the minor deviations of individual specimens. Archæologists have in practice proceeded not by grouping together ever wider assemblages of increasingly abstract types, but rather by subdividing such groups by discriminating ever more concrete types. How far can such discrimination profitably proceed? No general rule can be laid down *a priori*, but some practical hints may be deduced from concrete examples.

In 1912 Abercromby defined in the British Isles a

'Beaker' culture characterized by beakers, bronze daggers, tanged-and-barbed arrow-heads and burial under round barrows. He recognized indeed different types of Beaker, (labelled A, B and C), and of daggers associated with them, but treated these as members of typological series. In 1931 Clark and Grimes pointed out that B beakers and their associated daggers could hardly be derived from A beakers and their associates, that each type was in fact associated with independent assemblages and that if plotted on a map of sufficient size the B beaker group exhibited a different distribution to that of A and C beakers. Then in 1938 Piggott showed that B beakers in turn could be subdivided into B1 and B2 beakers, not derivable typologically one from the other and with discrepant associations and distributions. Thus B1, B2 and A–C beakers each became diagnostic of a distinct culture. Subsequently A and C beakers have been similarly separated. So in 1955 British prehistorians recognized four beaker cultures instead of one!

In the meantime the Continental Bell-beaker culture, from which Abercromby had shown in 1912 that his British Beaker culture must be derived, had likewise been subdivided, Zoned beakers and Veluwe beakers having been distinguished by form, technique and decoration, distribution and association, from the remaining Bell beakers. On the same criteria the British B1 beaker complex can be derived from the Continental Bell-beaker culture; it can in fact be treated as the British group of the Bell-beaker culture while our B1 beakers may be regarded as local variants of the Bell-beaker rather than as a distinct type. So in 1955 the Bell-beaker culture seems a convenient unit of chorological classification and the Bell-beaker a diagnostic type.

Now though local *variants* on this type can easily be distinguished in Britain, Brittany, the Rhineland, the Upper Elbe-Danube basins, the Pyrenæan region, Almeria and elsewhere, all share conspicuous common features in technique, form and decoration that are not replicated on British A beakers nor indeed on any other ceramic class. Moreover all the common formal features can be recognizably represented by a sketch which could not, however, do justice also to the distinctive peculiarities of British A beakers. In other words the Bell-beaker is capable of *ostensive definition*, and this definition would exclude other vases of the same family. Secondly, the Bell-beaker is everywhere and exclusively associated with a specialized type of metal dagger, equally definable by ostensive definition, and exclusively, though not universally, with a similarly defined bowman's wrist guard while other items of archers' equipment are everywhere associated with beakers, though the types of arrow-head vary locally. Thirdly, though Bell-beakers are very widely distributed in Europe, they do cluster in a few well-defined habitats. So to be diagnostic of a culture a type should be (1) capable of ostensive definition (its formal features being reproducible diagrammatically), (2) exclusively associated with two or more similarly definable types, and (3) distributed in accordance with a recognizable pattern.

Now if the generalized Bell-beaker be termed the *type*, the sort of Bell-beaker found exclusively in England, Brittany, Almeria or some other region will have to be called a *variant* and distinguished by a geographical adjective—e.g. Armorican or Pyrenæan. At the same time Zoned beakers, British A beakers and others do exhibit a family likeness to Bell-beakers and to one another, and do share some common associations too. They might then all be grouped together in a single *family*. It may be convenient to recognize still higher groupings that might be labelled species and classes. A second example will illustrate the suggested terminology.

Within the functional *class*, 'battle-axes', the highly polished and perforated stone weapons to which this term is sometimes confined, may perhaps be considered a *genus*. Among such stone battle-axes several families could be distinguished. Those in which the blade expands symmetrically on both sides of the weapon's long axis and those in which it expands only downwards or droops, constitute two well-recognized *families*. Neither constitutes a type; for in each family a bewildering variety reigns that could not be comprised in even a schematic drawing. But among the drooping battle-axes it is possible to recognize a certain number of types, the distinctive features of which could be adequately indicated in sketches, while each is concentrated in a well-defined habitat and frequently associated with several other equally concrete diagnostic types. These regional types are conveniently distinguished by an adjective that may be either descriptive ('faceted', 'boat-axe') or derived from the region where they cluster (Jutland, Saxo-Thuringian) or from the culture they help to define ('Fatyanovo').

In this case too we can distinguish regional variants on a battle-axe type, associated with corresponding variants in other diagnostic types. Such can conveniently be designated by a geographical term such as Čuvaš variant of the Fatyanova battle-axe. Rather greater deviation from the norm may distinguish consecutive phases of the same culture; indeed the deviation may be so great that a fresh definition or drawing is needed for the weapons characteristic of each phase, though their typological descent from the earlier type is usually obvious. Such variants are not, however, diagnostic of a distinct culture, only of a new phase in the development of one culture. It would be convenient not to give them new names, but to distinguish them by a chronological adjective or numeral; in Denmark the terms Ground Grave and Upper Grave are used and are really chronological. Finally two or three quite distinct types of battle-axe may be associated with indistinguishable types of other diagnostic traits in a single province; all equally characterize therefore one and the same culture and period. Such equivalent types are generally distinguished by a letter or numeral—e.g. Jutland Bottom Grave A (type) battle-axe. It will be convenient to postpone to the next chapter the interpretation of assemblages characterized by types of the same family and the nomenclature appropriate thereto.

Once two or three diagnostic types have been selected with the aid of the foregoing criteria for the recognition of a culture, the next step will be to enumerate all types and phenomena associated with them, including such traits as can be inferred from their distribution. Only then can the search for the behaviour patterns that unite and hold together all these disconnected traits profitably begin. Its discovery will be facilitated if the available data be exhaustively catalogued and arranged in a logical order (even if that arrangement involve the duplication of some entries). The following scheme is advanced tentatively as a basis for discussion without any claims to being exhaustive or even logical.

ECONOMY

I. PRIMARY ECONOMY

(A) Habitat (deduced from cartography and raw materials found).

(B) Food supply:

(1) Wild (bones of animals, fish, wild plant remains).

(2) Plant cultivation:

(i) plant remains; (ii) provisions for tilling soil (including fields and irrigation canals); (iii) harvesting; (iv) processing (querns, etc.); (v) storing; and (vi) cooking.

(C) Warmth and shelter:

(1) Heat and light:

(i) fuels; (ii) kindling appliances; (iii) hearths, ovens, lamps, etc.

(2) Dwellings:

(i) materials; (ii) plans; (iii) furniture.

(3) Clothing:

(i) actual remains and representations; (ii) textile and leather-dressing appliances; (iii) buttons, pins, etc.

II. INDUSTRIES

(A) Stone working:

(i) Selection; (ii) extraction; (iii) techniques of shaping; (iv) uses—for tools, weapons, vases, in building and art.

(B) Metallurgy:

(i) Metals used; (ii) extractive processes; (iii) manufacturing processes; (iv) extent of use.

(C) Bone, horn and ivory.
(D) Carpentry.
(E) Pottery and brick.
(F) Textiles and basketry.
(G) Hides.
(H) Other natural materials (salt, amber, jet).
(I) Other artificial materials.

III. TRANSPORT

(A) By water:
(i) vessels; (ii) means of propulsion (paddles, oars, sails); (iii) harbours and canals.

(B) By land:
(i) vehicles (sledge, travoise, cart); (ii) traction; (iii) roads and bridges.

IV. TRADE

(1) Imported raw materials and manufactures; exports.
(2) Hoards, trading posts.
(3) Trade routes.

V. WAR

(1) Offensive weapons, including war-chariots.
(2) Defensive constructions; armour.
(3) Remains of battles, destruction layers in settlements.

SOCIOLOGY

I. DEMOGRAPHY

(1) Size of settlements and cemeteries.
(2) Density of settlements.

II. FAMILY AS AN INSTITUTION

Size of houses, grouping within village, burial practices.

III. TOWN PLANNING

IV. STRUCTURE

Specialization of labour.
Stratification: differences in wealth, or rank.

IDEOLOGY

I. SCIENTIFIC

(A) Writing and numeral notation.
(B) Counting.
(C) Measurement (weights and measures).
(D) Geometry: construction of right angles, circles.
(E) Calendrical science: orientation.
(F) Medicine and surgery.

II. NUMENOLOGICAL

(A) Burial rites and tomb types.
(B) (i) temples and sanctuaries; (ii) figurines, idols, phalli; (iii) aniconic ritual objects.
(C) Rites—e.g. cannibalism, votive offerings.

III. ARTISTIC

(A) Graphic arts.
(B) Musical instruments.
(C) Personal adornments, including wigs, razors, tweezers, bath-tubs.

IV. SPORTIVE

(A) Knuckle-bones, dice, draughtsmen.
(B) Cursūs, ball-courts.
(C) Toys and rattles.

When a culture has been thus circumscribed in time and space and logically inventoried, can anyone say what sort of sociological group behaved thus? By definition the sociological unit concerned is larger than the local community, the inhabitants of a single cave or a single village; a number of sites scattered over a larger or smaller area all yield the same diagnostic types, so the inhabitants of all shared the common traditions and behaviour patterns. But to what sort of society must all these local communities belong to exhibit the observed uniformity of behaviour patterns? What shall we term the society that maintains the common tradition? Not a race; culture is transmitted by social, not biological channels, and as far as anthropometric data go, the bearers of the same culture do not normally exhibit the same anthropological physical type. Nor yet a political State; archæologists can recognize a Sumerian culture at a time when Sumer was divided into a number of independent and often hostile city-states. It can perhaps distinguish local variants, and distinguish the sphragistic of Ur from that of Kish or Mari, but the total pattern recognized archæologically displays an overriding unity and can be contrasted with that detected in Elam or North Syria. It is to be hoped that archæologists will similarly recognize a Greek culture, unifying all the little city-states. It is of course easy and essential to recognize Bœotian, Attic, Æginetan, Argive and other pottery styles, distinctive of as many independent *poleis*. But all are Greek and none could be mistaken for Egyptian, Phœnician or Phrygian. Similar divergences could be detected between the several cities in the domains of architecture, personal ornaments and so on, but always within an overriding community of types that could be equally contrasted to Levantine or Lydian. The archæologist need not lose the Greeks among the Bœotians, Athenians, Argives . . . !

So it would be impossible to doubt that Cyrene and Agrigentum were Greek cities even though no written documents guaranteed their colonial character. Similarly nineteenth-century Sydney or Geelong, despite its exotic setting, would be recognizable as a British colony. Conversely on archæological evidence alone a British settlement in the southern hemisphere will never be mistaken for a Kaffir kraal or an aboriginal camp. Just so in ancient Sicily the Greek colonies cannot be confused with hill-forts of the independent Sicels.

On the other hand the rule of ostensive definition should limit the denotation of the culture-name. Between these extremes the sociological counterpart of an archæological culture can only be designated by the non-committal term 'people'. That being so, preliterate cultures can only be distinguished by some quite conventional appellation. Prehistorians sometimes use the name of a diagnostic type for the culture it characterizes and so we have Bell-beaker culture, Boat-axe culture, Tumulus culture. More often cultures are called after sites where the distinctive assemblages were first recognized or are particularly well represented like Rinaldone, Windmill Hill or—in adjectival form, Aurignacian, Unĕtician. Students may find such place names hard to remember, but they are at least international. The type names of the former system, if more readily learnt by heart, have to be translated from language to language and are seldom neatly or exactly translatable. *Tragtbægrekultur* looks well enough in Danish while *civilisation des gobelets à étonnoire* is, to put it mildly, clumsy. *Srubnaya kul'tura* has a precise technical meaning in Russian very imperfectly rendered by *Holzbalkengräberkultur*. Designation by eponymous sites is today becoming the accepted standard and provided the same name is not applied to an archæological period (page 96) seems the most satisfactory. Occasionally a region instead of a site is taken as eponym, sometimes with a qualifying adjective—Lusatian, Saxo-Thuringian, Early Kuban, Danubian I. Established names of this type are likely to be retained, but no new ones have been adopted during the last twenty-five years. Terms like Iron Age A culture or Neolithic B culture are of course mere expedients that may prove temporarily convenient for purely local classification and description, but cannot be employed in any comprehensive work on prehistory.

CHAPTER EIGHT

What Happens in Prehistory?

HAVING rigged a culture up with the trappings of personality and set it on the stage of archæological history, what acts shall the archæologist present it performing? It should be exhibited developing, changing before the spectator's eyes. It may move about, and enter into relations with other cultures, but archæologically these too are just changes, changes in the distribution of the diagnostic types and changes in the composition of the assemblages they characterize or in those types themselves. Only the latter changes can strictly speaking be termed changes in culture or cultural changes though distributional changes may promote these.

Distributional changes should reflect displacements of population, the expansions, migrations, colonizations or conquests with which literary history is familiar. The simplest case may be termed expansion. Any population may be expected to multiply, but the new mouths can be fed only by exploiting new territory or by intensifying the productivity of the original habitat. Even on the second alternative, since the productivity of any area is limited, the population, if it continue to grow, must eventually overflow. On the other hand the human population of our globe was once exceedingly sparse—*Homo sapiens* was originally a rare animal. In prehistoric and even in early historical times immense tracts of land were totally or virtually uninhabited. Even in the European Middle Ages the gradual clearance of forests and appropriation of wastes by European peasantries was a familiar phenomenon; it continued for many centuries and must have begun millennia before the Roman Conquest.

Such gradual encroachment of humanity on the wilderness would theoretically be represented archæologically by a more or less continuous distribution of types, diagnostic of one culture round a primary nucleus. In so far as a typological development is detectable in these relics, the later stages should of course be more widely distributed than the earlier ones, but save in relatively recent times, technological progress has been far slower than the expansion of population.

In practice it would be hard to draw any logical distinction between this hypothetical expansion and colonization or migration. The distribution pattern is not really likely to be continuous, since regions where the favourite game was scarce or hard to catch, less fertile soils, patches of swamp or desert, bare rocks and rugged mountains will be avoided or passed over. So the distribution of find-spots will be interrupted by empty spaces.

If the search for a congenial habitat, whether hunting or fishing-grounds, cultivable soils, pastures or trading posts, involve traversing deserts, mountain ranges or stretches of sea, the migrants may quickly and even suddenly be brought into an environment diverging seriously from that of their starting-point. But even continuous expansion, if pushed far enough, would eventually bring the settlers into a novel environment. Now in so far as a culture is an adaptation to a specific environment, it must be modified by transfer to a different environment, and the degree of modification is likely to be inversely proportional to the culture's technological level. In no case can it be expected that one and the same culture should be represented by an identical assemblage of types in two contrasted environments. Conversely all cultures under identical environmental conditions are liable to exhibit quite a number of common traits—behaviour patterns and archæological types expressing them that are imposed on men by external natural conditions such as raw materials, or are at least adaptations peculiarly well fitted to securing survival in a particular environment. Step by step expansion, just as much as migration, is likely to bring a society into an habitat so different from its starting-point that adaptation to it will require an assemblage of types so different from those appropriate to the homeland that we seem to be confronted with distinct cultures. Fortunately for archæologists even quite progressive societies are often reluctant to relinquish cherished customs, however unsuitable they may have become. In Australia I remember in my youth eating turkey and plum pudding at Christmas when the temperature was over 95° F. and seeing judges walking through the blazing sun in black coats and top hats. In the southern hemisphere the traditional diet for a European Christmas was cherished and the dress then approved for an English gentleman remained obligatory.

Thus distributional change, as much as the lapse of

time, may result in cultural change, and in either case differentiation may proceed so far as to raise the question of the relation between two cultures. In principle there need be no difference between the cultural changes observed as one proceeds from the basal to the superficial layers of a stratified site and those distinguishing the starting and terminal points of an expansive or migratory movement. Both are presented in the archæological record as changes in the assemblage of types, the replacement or modification of old types and the emergence of quite novel ones. But in stratified sites, not all observed changes are changes in culture; they may be changes of culture. In other words the phenomena observed in successive layers may represent the replacement of one culture by another as much as the progressive development of a single culture. And not all the observed phenomena document cultural change at all. In an inhabited site we may discover a layer of ashes and debris reflecting the violent destruction of the whole settlement. The destruction layer records an historical event—a hostile attack or a natural catastrophe. The same or a parallel event may be recorded in homotaxial layers at several sites. Even so, the destruction is not itself a cultural change; it may be the prelude to one, but only if the assemblages from the re-occupation layers diverge from those beneath the debris.

No doubt all cultural changes, from a slight modification of a traditional pattern or deviation from a customary rite to a major invention like the wheel or a bold strategic innovation, originated with an individual who was naturally a member of a community. They are recognizable archæologically only if they have been adopted by, or imposed upon, a whole society. Recognizable changes in culture may be said to result from the internal genius of the society itself or to be provoked by some external event whether that be a change in the non-human environment or some sort of relation with another society.

The recognizable changes in culture whether between basal and superficial layers in a group of stratified sites or between the initial and terminal points of an expansive or migratory movement are presented in the archæological record as variations in assemblages of types and so could serve equally well as the bases for chorological as for chronological distinctions. In practice archæologists infer from observed divergences between assemblages from consecutive layers in one or more stratified sites either the development of one culture or the replacement of one culture by another. These opposing inferences are of course equivalent to the alternatives of peaceful internal development or military conquest. The former alternative is to be preferred on the following conditions: the distributions of the two assemblages should be concordant within the limits laid down on page 117; a substantial number of the new types distinguishing the later assemblages should be logically derivable from the old—ideally all the stages in typological series linking them should be discoverable locally. In this case, subject to reservations mentioned above, prehistorians do not regard the innovations in the upper layer as distinctive of a new culture nor apply a new name to the assemblages they characterize; they receive the same name as those from the lower levels but qualified by a numeral or chronological adjective as 'Magdalenian VI', 'Upper Solutrean', 'Middle Minoan'. If on the other hand sufficient typological continuity cannot be established between consecutive layers a change of culture is assumed and a new name introduced. As soon as adequate study showed that the types distinctive of consecutive layers in French caves could not logically be presented each as members of typological series, the old terms 'Lower', 'Middle' and 'Upper Aurignacian' were replaced by 'Perigordian I–II', 'Aurignacian' and 'Perigordian IV–V', or even by 'Chatelperronian', 'Aurignacian' and 'Gravettian'. In the Ægean this logical rule has been unhappily neglected. While Middle Minoan culture can plausibly be explained as a development and enrichment of Early Minoan culture and so called the middle stage in the development of Minoan culture, 'Middle Helladic culture' represents a sharp break in architecture, burial rites, pottery, personal ornaments and so on with 'Early Helladic' and ought to be given a distinct name.

When the distributions are discordant or exclusive—and such must result from expansive movements—a decision between the alternative interpretations is less easy. English culture of the twentieth century differs both from contemporary American culture and from sixteenth-century English culture. The last differed so superficially from sixteenth-century American culture, that the latter could be termed a colonial variant of English culture. So the contrast recognized today could be regarded as the result of divergent developments of one and the same culture in different environments. 'Environment' not being qualified by 'natural' includes relations to other cultures—Spanish, Dutch, French, Pre-Columbian—that markedly affected the development in the New World. When communications were more difficult, divergence between spatially separated groups must have proceeded faster and farther. Some early Neolithic cultures in Europe provide examples.

The earliest and simplest Danubian pot-forms and decorative patterns are replicated with surprising uniformity all over the löss-lands from the Bakony in Hungary to the Harz in central Germany and from the Vistula to the Meuse and are associated everywhere with equally uniform house types, stone adzes and personal ornaments. The settlements being confined strictly to the löss, the distribution is interrupted by considerable blank spaces, but is as continuous as it could possibly be, given that restriction on habitat. In the sequel in various parts of this territory the old ceramic repertoire of forms and patterns develops into divergent local styles, each associated, albeit in varying degrees, with parallel innovations in architecture, armament, burial rites and so on. Some of the latter innovations, associated with most local ceramic styles, appear as complete novelties while others are at least as clearly typological developments from the older inventory. The local divergence of ceramic styles then seems to denote the break up of one original Danubian culture into a family of new cultures. Provided these new ceramic styles be exclusively associated with two or three other equally differentiated diagnostic traits and exhibit definite and mutually exclusive distributions, each must be accepted as characterizing a distinct culture on the principles laid down on page 113 and now deducible from our Anglo-American parable. Consequently each culture thus characterized deserves a name of its own, however obvious be its descent from the original Danubian and consequently its status as a phase in that culture's development.

All these cultures may be considered *genetically* related, *directly* to the original Danubian, *colaterally* to one another. The totality of genetically related cultures constitutes the simplest case of what I propose to designate a *cycle* (of cultures) or culture-cycle. A more objective definition would be: All cultures, characterized by the same families of types (page 127), belong to the same cycle. If then the habitat of a culture be termed a *province*, let us say that cycles occupy *spheres*.

For the term cycle, now proposed, 'civilization' has been suggested instead. Yet, while 'civilization', like 'culture', can be used as a partitive sense, as for instance by Toynbee, it has also been used by sociologists for nearly two centuries to denote a stage in social evolution, contrasted to 'savagery' and 'barbarism'. It would be confusing to apply the term 'civilization' to a group of preliterate cultures, especially as writing is generally taken as the differentia of civilization. (Incidentally the distinction could not be conveyed in French where 'civilisation' is the correct translation for English 'culture'.) This objection would not apply to a group of cultures that have all attained literacy. 'Greek civilization' or 'Roman civilization' would denote a totality equal in rank to our Danubian cycle. It might indeed be better to speak of a Bœotian culture within Greek civilization rather than a Bœotian variant of Greek culture.

Pittioni[1] likewise recognizes a hierarchy of chorological divisions, but distinguishes more ranks and describes them differently. My 'cycle' he would term a 'world' (*Welt*), but he defines 'culture' (*Kultur*) by more abstract types than I suggest on page 128 and so

[1] *Vom geistigen Menschenbild der Urzeit*, Vienna, 1952.

can divide each up into several 'groups' (*Gruppen*) that generally approximate to my 'cultures' while my 'variants' approximate to what Pittioni calls 'types' (*Typen*). While his hierarchy may be the more logical, mine corresponds better to current international usage and will therefore cause less confusion to students who read other authors.

Our discussion of changes in the distribution of cultures, reflecting the movements of peoples, and of the consequent cultural changes, has thus brought us to relations between spatially distinct cultures, or rather to the specific kind of relation termed *genetic*. Most archæologists are so far diffusionists as to admit some relation between any two cultures which share even one reasonably improbable type. But that relation need not be genetic.

The first English trader who presented a bottle of gin and a necklace of beads to the chief of a Pacific Island, even though he had no successor, established a relation between the island culture and British civilization that archæologists could recognize if they could not define precisely. A regular repetition of such trading visits might not only multiply recognizable imports, but also lead to the replacement of stone adzes and shell knives by metal ones with an inevitable reaction on the art of wood carvers and perhaps some modification of native costume. The island culture would thus share several types with British and Australian cultures, but no archæologist would be tempted to infer the same sort of relation between the former and the latter as subsisted between the last two. The relation would be still patently external.

Japan, Australia and Britain are shown to be related by sharing quite a large number of highly improbable types like railways, textile factories and policemen's uniforms, and nearly all the types or families of types common to Japan and Australia before 1914 could be shown to have originated in and been derived from Britain. The industrialization of Japan and the 'westernization' of her police force did involve the temporary settlement there of expert operatives, engineers and instructors. But these temporary immigrants were not colonists, and formed a tiny minority in Japan's population. Though industrialization reacted on dress, architecture and several other facets of Japanese culture, it left its essential fabric intact. The relations of Japanese to Australian and British cultures were still different in kind from those subsisting between the Australian and the British, though all would be attested archæologically by the same types or by types of the same family. Only Australian-British relations should be described as genetic. And they would be attested by more common types and types different in kind. Japanese culture did not share with Australian those behaviour patterns expressed for instance in shower-baths, house-plans, golf-courses and churches that are common to Australia and Britain. It is these that disclose Australian culture as a local variant of British culture, or, if you will, a provincial variant of British civilization.

In comparing simpler societies (which are not likely to include craft groups of full-time specialists), archæologists may infer genetic relations, despite separation in space, from communities of arbitrary types that are the home-made products of domestic industries or ideological behaviour rather than from types that have been imported, produced by specialized crafts or are imposed by their superior efficiency or by environmental circumstances. Imported manufactures or raw materials, as such, are obviously irrelevant. Even among preliterate societies, specialists such as metal workers or tile-makers may leave one community to work for another; inventions that enhance efficiency like the rotary quern or the cut-and-thrust sword can be communicated from one society to another with even less interchange of personnel than textile factories and police helmets; any society that moved into the treeless Orkney islands would have to translate its traditional wooden houses and furniture into stone. So good indicators of genetic connexion between two spatially separated cultures should be (1) home-made, (2) peculiar to the cultures to be related, and (3) not environmentally conditioned. But at least two traits thus qualified are requisite for any plausible inference and the inference would remain very provisional unless further common types can be identified.

Hand-made pots seem to conform ideally to the above requirements because they are not suitable for transport for any distance and therefore for trade articles and moreover are believed—on ethnographic analogies—to be normally made by women who are reputedly more conservative than men. Nevertheless pots, though not themselves likely to be traded, often imitate vessels of more valuable and portable material such as metal. Indeed, in the Early Bronze Age of many parts of Asia and Europe painted and incised decoration went out of fashion in pottery, and vases were given a plain burnished surface as if to mimic metal ware.[1] Textiles, if they survived, should fulfil the same conditions quite as well and, though actual fabrics hardly ever survive, a specialized textile equipment

1 Schachmayr, in *Archiv. f. Orientforschung*, XVI, 1952–3, p. 86.

may be equally illuminating. A concrete example of this use of textile equipment may be quoted to set beside the Danubian expansion traced mainly with the age of pottery.

In 1935[1] I suggested that the 'Broch culture' of northern Scotland should be derived from South-western England on the strength of the exact correspondence of the textile appliances and of the dice from brochs with the types found at Glastonbury and other sites of the 'South-western B culture'. In 1949 Sir Lindsay Scott[2] demonstrated equally close and striking agreements in house-plans and pottery between the assemblages from the two regions. Of course the assemblages from the brochs lack many of the refinements, such as artistic metalwork and even the finer ceramic decoration, found in South-western England, while peculiarities have developed as adaptations to the new environment; stone for instance replaced wood. That in no wise impairs the direct genetic relation between the two cultures. It gives proof of an actual colonization of the Isles and North Scotland from South-west England as conclusive as archæologists can ever hope to offer.

The expansion of early Danubian culture, as sketched on page 141, led by divergent local developments to the emergence of a cycle of collateral cultures. Direct relation to a single ancestral culture seems the most obvious way of explaining the relations between cultures sharing several families of types of the kind indicative of genetic relations when direct descent of the several types from one another is impossible. Such cycles are common enough, but all too often the

[1] *Prehistory of Scotland*, London, 1935.
[2] 'Gallo-British Colonies', *P.P.S.*, XIV, 1948, pp. 46–125.

common ancestor remains a postulate. In northern Holland, Jutland, Denmark, Central Germany (Saxo-Thuringia), Silesia, Sweden, with the east Baltic coasts and Central Russia we find cultures all characterized by local types of battle-axes of the same family with downward drooping blades (page 127) associated in each case with four or five types from six equally distinctive families. These cultures are usually grouped together as a single cycle and termed 'the battle-axe cultures'. Admittedly neither drooping-bladed battle-axes nor any other single type of the remaining five families are exclusively associated with cultures of this cycle, but in no culture outside the battle-axe cycle are types of so many of the six families associated together. The simplest way of accounting for the observed agreements between the six cultures is to regard all as derived by local divergence from a single 'Battle-axe culture' spread by the migrations of a single 'Battle-axe folk'. So far, however, no such ancestral culture has been identified, and, until it be, the 'Battle-axe people' remain a highly speculative postulate.

It should indeed be remembered that cultural change may result in convergence as well as divergence and that in historical times the formation of what we may term British or French culture was due not to the differentiation of a local culture out of a wider cultural continuum, but to the assimilation of a series of already differentiated local cultures. Russian archæologists would explain in some such way the rise of the Andronovo culture in South-western Siberia and Kazakhastan. Over this vast area uniform assemblages characterized by a very distinctive ceramic style and scarcely less distinctive metal types succeed a multitude of small but easily distinguishable local cultures, while the diagnostic Andronovo types do not seem derivable from any one of the earlier local cultures rather than another nor from any one known culture outside their area. So the observed cultural unification is interpreted by some Russian authors as the reflexion of a federation of autonomous local groups, by others as the consequence of the adoption by such groups of stock-breeding, agriculture and metallurgy.[1] Nevertheless cultural assimilation and unification has in historical times been effected by the absorption of one or more cultures by another. Normally some recognizable types of the absorbed cultures survive locally. In that case the process of absorption produces hybrid cultures which are genetically related as colaterals.

We have in fact assumed that the distributional changes in the cultures whose expansion was discussed on page 141 were taking place in a human and cultural vacuum. That very seldom was true. Usually the expanding or migrating societies in the end came up against other societies with distinct cultures. On reaching the territory occupied by the others the migrants may halt. In this case the distributions of the types distinctive of the two cultures should when mapped, reveal a recognizable frontier between two provinces as explained on page 118. Thus, for instance, in south-west Finland[2] the distribution of boat-axes discloses a sharp frontier between the intrusive battle-axe farmers and the older hunter-fishers who made comb-ornamented pottery. Alternatively the immigrants may advance into the other people's territory, into a

[1] Formozov, 'O Proiskhozhdeniĭ Andronovskoĭ kul'tury', *K.S.*, XXXIX, 1951, pp. 1–15; Tolstov, *Drevniĭ Khorezm*, Moskva, 1948, pp. 66–8.

[2] A. Äyräpää, in *Suomen Museo*, LIX, 1952, pp. 18–25.

different cultural province. In this case they may either drive out or exterminate the former occupants and so extinguish the previous culture of the province. Or they may subdue or fuse with the former occupants.

In the first case the archæological result will be the replacement of the former culture of the province by the intrusive culture—the most drastic form of cultural change that may be observed in a stratified site (page 140). In the second the consequence will appear in the formation of a *mixed culture*, characterized by types derived from both components and genetically related to each. In such a hybrid when the intrusive types predominate over those previously characteristic of the province, prehistorians are inclined to speak of dominance or conquest and to assign the composite culture to the cycle to which the predominant types belong. In the reverse, they may use the term absorbtion.

Estimates of dominance are liable to be highly subjective, its interpretation in 'political' terms as conquest is always speculative. When the two cultures are on different technological levels, the more efficient types expressive of such superiority will almost inevitably predominate in the resultant mixed culture. So when barbarians conquer a civilized province, their political and military success may scarcely be registered in the archæological record. Again in so far as one culture is a good adaptation to an environment, the adaptive types will be taken over and preserved by an intrusive culture that had been adapted to a different environment. In this case too invaders, though most probably also conquerors, are likely to appear to archæologists to have been absorbed.

Quite often the culture of the invaded region is both technically superior to and better adapted to the environment than that of the invaders. So both factors combine to promote the predominance of the native types. This is what makes it so hard to detect archæologically the invaders from the temperate forest zone who in the course of history have so often conquered parts of the more civilized Mediterranean world. Hence in Lombardy Lombard culture looks more Roman than Teutonic, even more than Frankish culture in France appears predominantly Gallo-Roman.

In fact the ultimate and historically most significant consequence of conquest is the formation of a mixed culture, normally richer than either of the components and usually more progressive. If the immediate result be the imposition of an upper class ruling over a subject population, the best hope of recognizing the latter is from their graves; the burial ritual, the weapons and personal ornaments buried with the deceased in some graves may be contrasted not only with those previously current in the province but also with those of other contemporary graves. In the Usatova culture of the Pontic steppe the mass of the types from domestic sites could logically be interpreted as adaptive developments of the Tripolye culture with some borrowings from neighbouring 'steppe' or battle-axe cultures. The contrast of a few burials under large barrows accompanied by human sacrifices and predominantly 'steppe' pottery and weapons with cemeteries of flat graves in which pottery painted in the Tripolye technique predominates, seems to prove that the 'steppe' elements in the Usatova culture are really due to a fusion between Tripolye peasants and Steppe pastoralists and that the latter enjoyed social and political pre-eminence over the cultivators. Again in cemeteries of the Bylany culture of Bohemia[1] the contrast between the majority of rather poorly furnished cremation graves in the established Urnfield tradition and a few burials by inhumation accompanied by wheeled hearses, weapons and rich grave-goods clearly reflects the imposition of a military aristocracy upon an established Urnfield population; indeed by this time in the Iron Age it may be possible to distinguish within the latter 'kings' and their 'knights'.

Such unambiguous cases are very exceptional. Fusion need not necessarily lead to the formation of a society stratified into ruling and subject classes. Even if it does, there remains the horrid possibility that the subjects received no ceremonial burial at all, so that only the aristocracy would be represented in the archæological record, but could not be recognized as such for lack of contrast with 'commoners' or subjects! Archæologists have been too prone to 'explain' cultural change by migrations or conquests and to interpret all relations between cultures as genetic, in the hope it would seem of disguising prehistory in the semblance of nineteenth-century politico-military history. Recent instances cited on pages 143–4 have already shown that not all relations between cultures are genetic in the foregoing sense and not all typological communities are to be explained in 'political' terms.

When two peoples are spatially juxtaposed, when, that is, the archæological types diagnostic of the two cultures, respectively plotted on a map, exhibit exclusive distributions, archæologically recognizable relations will almost inevitably be established between them. These may take the form of a mere interchange

[1] Dvořak, '*Knížec Pohrby na Vozech*, Praha, 1938.

of products, recognizable by stray types of the one culture on the territory of the other and, at least when associated with types proper to the latter, conventionally interpreted as 'trade'. Secondly types of one culture may be adopted by its neighbour. In southwest Finland beyond the frontier dividing the boat-axe farmers from the hunter-fishers (page 148) and on the territory of the latter some boat-axes do occur. These, being made in the materials and by the techniques proper to the hunter-fishers, are easily distinguishable from the farmers' products and identifiable as copies of alien forms. But on a few hunter-fisher encampments, located near the frontier, some pots, decorated with cord-impressions in the style of the farmers, were manufactured as well as the native comb-impressed vessels. Äyräpää[1] has plausibly explained this phenomenon as a result of intermarriage between the two distinct societies. In both cases we have positive instances of *acculturation* without any political fusion or domination—a phenomenon exemplified by British-Japanese relations as quoted on page 144, and illustrated just as clearly by the contacts between the Greek colonists on the Sicilian coasts and native tribes in the interior and again all along the frontiers of the Roman Empire. When the cultures concerned are relatively poor in distinctive archæological types, the results of such external contact could easily be mistaken for mixed cultures and as indicative of genetic relations to the component cultures.

In their reaction against an exaggerated appeal to migrationist explanations and their abuse to further the ends of German imperialism, Russian prehistorians for a time tended to deny migrations and

[1] See note 2, page 148.

conquests altogether and so to rule out genetic relations between prehistoric cultures. This sort of approach in fact obliges the prehistorian to undertake a much profounder study of the cultures concerned than is demanded for facile migrationist interpretations and so leads to a deeper appreciation of neglected aspects of the data. Krichevskiĭ's[1] brilliant essay on the so-called 'Nordic cultures' in Central Europe illustrates this point well. The agreements among the several Late Neolithic cultures of the Danubian province both with one another and with those of Northern Europe had traditionally been explained by German prehistorians as resulting from conquests of the löss lands by successive bands of warlike invaders from the North European plain. Krichevskiĭ proposed to account for the general resemblances between the Central and North European cultures by the undoubted fact that in Late Neolithic times there was a general shift in emphasis from tillage to stock-breeding that had actually proved the more productive pursuit under the prevailing environmental and technological conditions; the rest of the observed changes would be more or less ideological reflexions of the economic revolution. To document this thesis he was able to show that far more of the types, distinctive of the Late Neolithic cultures, could be reasonably derived from those current in the province, albeit in rather embryonic forms and previously neglected, during the Middle Neolithic stage. This documentation at least represented a substantial contribution to knowledge, even if the author's thesis cannot be accepted in its entirety on factual and methodological grounds.

1 'Indogermanskiĭ vopros arkheologicheski razreshennyĭ', in *Izvestiya* GAIMK., 100, Moskva, 1935.

This contrast between Russian Marrist (not Marxist!) and German imperialist interpretations is after all just a special case of the controversy between evolutionists and diffusionists that has divided ethnographers as well as archæologists for the last fifty years and that raged with unusual fury in the English-speaking world in the twenties. Extreme adherents of both schools have become sectaries and converted their respective hypotheses into irreconcilable but undemonstrable dogmas. But in so far as evolutionism and diffusionism are heuristic principles, prehistorians should be at the same time both evolutionists and diffusionists.

On the one hand, observed changes in the archæological record from any one province should be explained as far as possible by reference to the local data. That is, innovations in each period should, wherever possible, be treated as developments of tendencies discoverable in the previous period. So assemblages from the latter should be closely scrutinized with a view to finding therein embryonic precursors of the new types and the intermediate stages in typological series linking these to the old. Gratuitously to invoke migrations or 'influences' from outside may be a mere cloak for laziness and has the effect of relegating to the wings all the action of the prehistoric drama.

On the other hand, a single type common to two cultures, however remote, establishes a presumption that some sort of relation subsisted between them and is thus a challenge to prehistorians to demonstrate this relation and clarify its nature. A type is the concrete embodiment of an idea, so the same type at two points in space or in time should document the diffusion of an idea on the useful heuristic hypothesis that each invention has been made but once. Of course no archæological evidence could rigorously demonstrate the diffusion of an idea. It can prove opportunities for diffusion and it can enhance the probability that diffusion in a specific case has taken place.

Intercourse, carrying with it opportunities for the communication and diffusion of ideas between two provinces and their inhabitants, is irrefutably attested by the transportation of natural substances far from the places where they occur in nature. Documented already in the Upper Palæolithic stage by Mediterranean shells in Central France and the vertebræ of Atlantic fish in caves in the Riviera, such intercourse notoriously became ever more frequent and of wider scope in subsequent archæological periods. From the Neolithic stage onwards manufactured articles of specialized types afford equally reliable evidence. Opportunities for diffusion and external relations between cultures can thus be rigorously proved, but only under rather exceptional circumstances or within a narrow geographical range.

To enhance the probability of diffusion distributional, quantitative and qualitative criteria may be invoked. The nearer together the find-spots of a single type be, the less likely is it that the type in question was invented or devised independently at each.

(1) When the challenge comes from two remote sites, a first response should be to look for specimens in intermediate regions. In the third millennium B.C. double-spiral headed-pins are found both in Greece and in the Indus valley. The probability that the type was diffused from one region to the other or to both from a third centre has been enhanced by the discovery of examples in Turkey, Turkmenia and Persia.

(2) The more types that are common to two sites or cultures, the less likely it is that any or all of them arose independently in each region. Having found one common type or trait we should therefore look for others. By 1300 B.C. chariots on four-spoked wheels were driven by warriors both in China and in Central Europe. When it appeared that in both regions they were drawn by horses, often interred in 'royal tombs' and regularly associated with socketed celts of tin-bronze, the inference to direct or indirect connexion between these two widely separated cultural provinces became virtually inevitable.

(3) The more improbable a type be, the more improbable is its independent invention two or more times. But probability cannot be determined *a priori* or by inspection (page 37). A type that is absolutely rare or that is confined to regions between which relations have been suggested by the previous criteria, may rank as improbable. Greater significance may be attached to double spiral-headed pins when it is remarked that such pins were not worn in Mesopotamia, Palestine or Syria in the third millennium nor in the Western Mediterranean and Temperate Europe till the second.

Archæologists can thus go quite a long way towards proving diffusion—but only of concrete types and specific patterns of behaviour. The diffusion of wheat-cultivation is in fact proven; for all cultivated wheats are derived from two species of wild grasses with a quite restricted distribution in South-west Asia; cultivated in Europe or China wheats constitute a case of 'the transportation of a natural substance far from the places where it occurs in nature'. It would be vain to try and prove 'the diffusion of agriculture'. 'The diffusion of the wheel' might provoke interminable controversies and appeals to contradictory abstract arguments. Substitute for 'the wheel', 'tripartite disk wheels' or 'four-spoked wheels' and the foregoing criteria can be invoked. These terms denote concrete types, definable by ostensive definition and capable of plotting on a map; no figure will adequately represent all the varieties of 'the wheel' actually known from the archæological record.

Indeed a fourth and virtually conclusive criterion is potentially available to establish almost conclusively the diffusion of such concrete types. If only the chronological framework be sufficiently comprehensive and the individual finds fixed in it closely enough, the earliest find-spots should be arranged along consecutive *isochrons* round the focus where the type originated. (An isochron, like an isobar or an isohyet, is just a line joining up find-spots on the map to which the same date relative or absolute is assigned.) In other words, the farther a region be from the centre where the type was invented, the later should be its first appearance (naturally the distance must not be measured in abstract units, but by reference to the effective communications established). Such distribution maps would not only provide the most conclusive evidence for diffusion imaginable, but would also define in what culture, i.e. among which people, the diffused idea originated. Yet it must always be remembered that the distributional pattern disclosed on such maps is liable to distortion by the differential capacities of local cultures to accept and incorporate what diffusion offers.

A culture-trait cannot be diffused to another culture unless it harmonizes with the latter's pattern. A culture is not like a formless pin-cushion into which a new invention, a novel rite or a fresh fashion can just be stuck. They just will not stay in place unless they fit organically into the highly complex but always flexible structure of the recipient. Double-spiral headed-pins will not be worn by people whose traditional costume or coiffure does not require any pins at all! So they were in fact not adopted in Crete or Egypt (page 155). Wheeled carts were not needed in the narrow valley of the Nile where the river, never far away, offered far more economical means of transport for heavy goods; in fact wheeled vehicles were not adopted in Egypt till more than a thousand years after their first use in Mesopotamia, and then as war-engines rather than transport devices. There is no use turning out *en masse* cheap pots on the wheel until population be dense enough to provide a local market to consume such fragile articles!

So the degree of proneness to adopt foreign ideas when exposed thereto by diffusion must itself rank as a significant item in a culture's description, just as the results will enrich the inventory of culture-contents. At the same time diffusion establishes a relation between cultures. But the precise nature of this relation, that is, the mechanism of diffusion, has to be inferred from the archæological data in each concrete case; traders, raiders, missionaries, conquerors, wives, colonists, imported slaves, returned mercenaries and many others may have been the agents.

CHAPTER NINE

What is the Good of Archæology?

IN the last four chapters and right to the end we have been pigeon-holing diagnostic fossils in chorological racks, shuffling carded types into chronological series and sprinkling dots on maps to make exclusive distributions. After all these arid pages of technicalities, an historian might well wonder what has happened to the ideas and human behaviour that he was promised. No doubt in brief interludes a layer of ashes has been rekindled to the flames of a ravaged citadel, a group of dots has been quickened into a band of peasants burning their way through virgin forest or a corroded dagger has evoked a party of mariners bartering arms and trinkets with barbarian natives on the sheltered shore of a Cornish bay. But that is hardly the kind of history promised. Of course, in this book we did not undertake to present history, but only the methods for extracting history from archæological data. Yet something should be said to dispel the disillusionment our excessively abstract account of those methods may produce.

To distil any sort of history from the surviving

archæological scraps the tedious processes of abstraction and classification were as essential as the equally tedious processes of excavation and conservation. The result was to be a panorama of human history ten thousand times wider than that reflected in written records and at the same time disembarrassed of irrelevant 'accidents' and temporary distortions. In such a scene any directional trend, any overriding pattern should stand out undisturbed by casual aberrations, any uniformities should be recognizable. Do any vistas open up in the landscape thus bared that can be briefly described?

Technological progress is of course conspicuous. In the one direction of control over external nature men have been extending their capacities for half a million years. But it was hardly necessary to climb an archæological peak to see beyond the depressions that have undoubtedly interrupted this ascent. Yet from this exceptional vantage point it is worth while glancing back along the upward track. Technological progress results from the accumulation of practical inventions and discoveries. It results in the multiplication of actions men can successfully execute, of processes they can direct, of gadgets they can use and of objects they can make therewith. In archæological terms that is equivalent to a multiplication of types, which is precisely the archæological proof of technical progress. Despite the horrifying gaps in the record, in each successive archæological period each successive culture is, apart from statistically insignificant deviations, richer than the one before, each, that is, is characterized by a greater number and a wider variety of distinguishable types.

Admittedly not all the new types added in each age

and period are technological devices; not all innovations demonstrably tend in the one direction of increased efficiency. Not all the novelties enable men to act more successfully on the external world. So not all observed changes can without question be qualified as progressive. Critics may debate whether Celtic artists in Western Europe in the second century B.C. could depict animals better than Magdalenian artists in the twelfth millennium. Æsthetically we may admit no progress. Yet one fact stands beyond dispute. The Celtic artists could and did produce more artistic types; they executed a greater number of motives in a wider variety of media. Similarly to speak of the efficiency of personal ornaments is meaningless, and estimates of their æsthetic merit will vary. Funerary furniture from successive periods reflects—rather imperfectly—an increase in the number and variety of pins, bracelets, anklets, necklaces, earrings, finger-rings and other articles of finery available. Even in the case of the relics and monuments disparagingly dubbed 'ritual' a like proliferation is detectable.

Now every type of whatever kind is the outcome of an act and the expression of an idea (page 75). Every addition to the repertoire of types therefore means an extension of the variety of actions successfully applied to the external world, and at the same time an enrichment of the stock of ideas constituent of thought or mind. 'Mind' cannot be regarded as a highly complicated machine composed of ready made parts into which sensations or percepts are fed to be ground out as actions and ideas. It is rather constituted by its contents. If so, any enrichment of content will be correlated to an enrichment of output. No agreed standards exist for judging the quality of thought.

Archæology can prove that it has grown richer, if not better. But the thought whose enrichment the archæological record documents is not the private thoughts of individuals but thoughts realizable in action and shared by all members of a society. Thoughts rejected by society and unrealizable, have been erased from the archæological record. They had proved idle fancies, vain imaginings.

The enrichment of thought documented archæologically is the growth of a world of ideas, or at least of worlds of ideas. No world is presented ready made in sensory perception. The world on which a man plans rational action and can act successfully is the world known to the society to which he belongs, a world of knowledge. That knowledge is not a mere reflexion of sense data, but a reconstruction of such data in the light of society's collective experience and ordered in accordance with its traditional logic. (I do not of course mean that the individual knower carries in his own head all the collective experience of his society nor that the rules of logic have to be formulated before they can be applied.)

In the Pleistocene period the world, as twentieth-century European scientists know it, contained rather more available carbon, copper and uranium than it does today. Yet the world known to Palæolithic hunters contained none of these elements at all. For them no environment offered even rich pastures nor fertile arable lands. These aspects were literally added to the environment by the Neolithic Revolution as coal was to be by the Industrial Revolution. The gold of Ballarat and the silver of Broken Hill did not exist for the aboriginal tribes of Australia. They were literally discovered by European prospectors just because gold and silver had each an appropriate place in the known world of nineteenth-century Europeans. Yet the Aborigines' failure to observe the metal and the ore was due to no inferiority in their bodily sense organs and neurological equipment, but only to deficiencies in their social equipment for interpreting what they saw, touched and tasted. *οἳ πρῶτα μὲν βλέποντες, ἔβλεπον μάτην κλύοντες οὐκ ἤκουον.*

Archæologists very properly invoke the aid of geologists, botanists and other natural scientists to reconstitute the environments of ancient societies. Prehistorians must always remember that what natural science reconstructs is not the environment to which its ancient inhabitants could or did adapt themselves. That was conditioned and limited by the patterns of observation, as well as of acting, traditional in the society. Herein lies the specific difference between the environment of *Homo sapiens* and that of *Helix nemoralis* or even *Felis leo*. The effective environment can be reconstructed only with the aid of the archæological evidence as to what the population actually did with it and in it. An exposure of neglected opportunities and consequently of the limitations on the exploiting society's technical and intellectual equipment should be not the least valuable contribution from natural science to human prehistory.

Archæology can demonstrate an enlargement of the world known to each society. That would be an enlargement of the known world only in so far as societies could and did pool acquired information. What our record reveals is an absolute increase in the total number of types produced by men in the course of archæological time. But this increase appears at once as accumulation and differentiation. The tripartite disk wheel was an addition to the means of land transport available. The number of types of wheeled vehicle was increased by the divergent application of the invention to different local types of sledge and also by the subsequent differentiation of farm-carts, war-chariots, ceremonial cars and so on. Lifelike portrayal of the human form represented an addition to the artists' repertoire at the Urban Revolution. Styles of portraiture diverged and therefore multiplied.

Even in technology progress towards enhanced mastery of external nature has not proceeded along parallel lines, but along divergent paths which only occasionally converged again. A winged axe, a Northern palstav and a Bohemian palstav was each an improvement on the flat celt but along divergent lines. All three in the end had to give place to the socketed celt. In domestic architecture, in dress and personal adornment, in artistic styles and in rituals divergence has been the principal factor in the multiplication of types. It is just this divergence that has made possible the chorological division of the archæological record and the recognition in prehistory of distinct societies. What archæologists observe and describe are not changes in culture, but changes in cultures.

The combination of chorological and chronological classifications in the structure of the archæological record permits an objective verdict on conflicting theories based on deductions from comparative ethnography. By analysing and comparing the arts and crafts, the social institutions, numenological beliefs and rituals of contemporary backward peoples, the Spencerian evolutionists sought to document an hypothesis of unilineal social evolution according to which all peoples on Earth were advancing along parallel roads, albeit at different rates, to a single goal that was almost realized in Victorian liberalism. From just the same data and by like comparative methods the Austrian diffusionists tried to reclothe in 'scientific' garb the old romantic notion of 'the Noble Savage' and the older theological dogma of 'the Fall of Man'.

In the comfort and quiet of donnish studies and monkish cells the quaint tastes, disgusting habits, odd fancies and ingenious expedients of backward heathen as reported by missionaries, traders, blackbirders and soldiers were scrupulously classified and indexed. By selecting, a trifle capriciously, the right card from these well-stocked files, weapons and marital relations, numinous powers and fashions of dress could be arranged in logically unimpeachable series to illustrate an 'evolution' from clubs to howitzers, from promiscuity to strict monogamy, from magic to monotheism, from waist strings to trousers. The logical series were then converted into historical sequences and arranged in parallel columns to document the Evolution of Society through consecutive stages. With a synchronic approach, limited to contemporary societies, such theories might remain exempt from any factual criticism. The archæological record alone allows of a diachronic approach. It reveals series that are also sequences in time and many such series observed in different environments and places concretely displaying the fortunes of distinct societies. A comparison of such series and sequences does not reveal parallelism at any significant level of abstraction, but rather divergence often modified by convergence, as indicated above.[1]

[1] I have collected and set forth some data in my *Social Evolution*.

If archæological data do not confirm the hypothesis of unilineal evolution, while they do suggest means for its rectification, the same evidence is even less compatible with dogmas of diffusion, based upon a similar confusion between logical sequence and temporal succession. The Austrian diffusionists of the Culture-Historical School do indeed frankly admit technological progress. But, they claim, every advance due to applications of fruit from the Forbidden Tree has been correlated with a step backwards in the moral sphere from the primal state of Primitive Innocence—at least until the Redemption.[1]

Of course a scheme of moral values is less likely to command universal assent than standards of utility, and archæologists could not hope to detect the monotheism, the strict observance of monogamous sexual relations and the scrupulous respect for private property that are supposed to have characterized Primitive Innocence till the Fall. Some of its evil results are less elusive; the consequent perversion and degradations of human conduct, as specified by Culture-historians themselves, are positively attested far too early for the latters' scheme. For instance, indisputable cases of homicide can be quoted from the Middle Palæolithic; by the same period and, at Chou-kou-tien perhaps still earlier, we have undeniable instances of cannibalism, certainly socially sanctioned and probably already ritual. The subjugation of women is illustrated by *sati* burials at least by the Mesolithic. In short archæology provides no evidence for an increase in antisocial behaviour nor for a decline in

[1] The theological implications of the Kulturhistorsiche Methode are revealed with engaging naïvety in O. Kern's review of Menghin's *Weltgeschichte der Steinzieit* in *Archiv f. Kulturgeschichte*, XXXII, 1931.

moral standards if it offer no more evidence for their progressive elevation. Such glimpses into the life of Palæolithic men as are afforded by Chou-kou-tien, Grimaldi and La Ferrassie suggest that their life was not only short and brutish but also—from the standpoint of a twentieth-century European—morally nasty.

As for the extreme English diffusionist thesis—'Savages never invent or discover anything'—it is flatly contradicted by both ethnographic and archæological facts. Not only were the most fundamental and difficult inventions and discoveries—ignition, the bow, the cultivation of cereals, the domestication of cattle, and so on—made before any society at all had attained civilization, their most important sequels like the spoked wheel, iron-smelting and the socketed celt, all arose outside the pale of the great oriental civilizations among still illiterate barbarians of the Bronze Age.

The archæological refutation of diffusionist dogmas is by no means equivalent to a denial of diffusionism. On the contrary that very increase in the totality of types that signifies for us the enrichment of thought (page 161) can be shown to be correlative to, if not causally dependent on, a comparable extension of the range, and intensification in the frequency, of intercourse between distinct societies. And intercourse means the diffusion of ideas. Archæology unaided by texts can of course prove only opportunities for intercourse. These are conclusively documented by the transportation of substances far from the localities where they occur naturally and by the distribution of manufactures of known provenance. Not only are such opportunities demonstrated over progressively longer distances for each successive period or age. An even more conspicuous multiplication of the volume of such 'trade' bears witness to a growing frequency and intensity of intercourse. In the Old Stone Age a few pierced shells thus reached the Dordogne from the Mediterranean coasts. By the beginning of our era the sea-shells transported, perhaps by the silent trade, a few hundred miles had grown into the ship-loads of Roman manufactures and Indian spices regularly wafted across the Arabian Sea by the monsoons to peninsular India and back again. Of course such regular seasonal voyaging implies that ships' captains and crews had hosts at Arakamedu and Berenice with whom they could live and converse while they awaited the wind favourable to the return voyage.

Incidentally extension of communication involved a widening of geographical knowledge, a spatial enlargement of the worlds of the communicating societies. Of societies, not individuals. Citizens and subjects of the Roman Empire residing in Britain would have known no more of the Indian Subcontinent than Queen Victoria's native subjects on Queen Charlotte's Sound or Arnhem Land. Yet India, its products and its demands, were incorporated in the world known to the Roman Empire as in that known to the late British Empire.

The refutation or even the rectification of speculative or obscurantist theories is perhaps a rather negative contribution to world history. But other issues of the kinds just illustrated, are susceptible of empirical examination and objective appraisal only with the aid of archæological data, though not until such data be fuller and more processed. For instance, we have the impression that in prehistoric as much as in historic times rates of cultural change, of technological progress have fluctuated. Can such fluctuations be correlated with other variables, such as the intensity of intercourse with other societies? Till an agreed absolute chronology permit us to measure the durations of archæological periods, we cannot even talk of rates of progress, still less compare them with other variables.

In any case it would be irrelevant in a book on methods to attempt a summary of conclusions. No plea of irrelevance could excuse at least a statement of the challenge to historical knowledge inherent in the relativity dilemma, though that statement may involve a 'metaphysical' excursus. Even the physicist has to recognize that the fact of observation may alter what should be observed. That is much more true for social scientists. Archæologists want to observe culture, but the instruments they must use, the categories of logic themselves, are part of culture. As an historian, the archæologist is bidden to re-enact in his own mind the thoughts and motives of the prehistoric agent. That might present no insuperable difficulty to a naïve realist nor to an old-fashioned idealist. If all 'minds' be passive reflectors of a single external world or, being cast in the same mould, automatically produce the same ideas from that external world, there is no problem. But these naïve attitudes have been empirically refuted.

Idealists too who believe in an absolute and transcendent Reason and such realists as imagine that the 'laws of thought' and the categories of logic are universal, eternal and prior to all experience, can afford to ignore the dilemma. But their assumptions also have been effectively challenged by the sociology of knowledge. The categories whereby 'Reason' reduces to order the data of sense perception are not found to be universal and immutable. They too have developed in the course of history and vary from society to society today. These variations, documented by Marx from written history and by Durkheim from ethnography, can be observed today in the exact sciences themselves. The President's address to the Physics Section of the British Association in 1938 was devoted to explain how logic had to be changed to accommodate an accumulation of data!

If then prehistoric men not only perceived different external worlds to what the twentieth century archæologist perceives, but also ordered their perceptions according to different categories, how can we know the world they knew, how re-enact in our own minds their thoughts? To be more concrete can we infer the thoughts of a Palæolithic flint-knapper from his products? Pittioni has argued that the systematic repetition of the same movements, quite reliably inferred from the successful production of thousands of standardized artifacts, discloses a knowledge of the 'law of cause and effect'. Do we not share that knowledge?

'Knowledge of causality' used perhaps to mean 'the belief that there is always an event A that is invariably followed by an event B'. Now there is written evidence that even a literate Sumerian only four thousand years ago conceived of flint as more like a person with characters than a substance with attributes. Evidently the Sumerian could not have formulated his concept of causality in anything like the above turns. Still less could a Moustierian forty thousand years ago. Plainly it is as impossible to recapture the thoughts that the Moustierian would have expressed in verbal symbols as to recover the verbal symbols he doubtless used.

This negative conclusion is due to a misconception

of the function of rational thought and of the nature of scientific laws. The function of reason is not contemplation, but action. A scientific law is not just a description of what happens but also the basis for a prescription for doing something. Even Pythagoras' Theorem provides a rule for making a right angle. A causal law becomes then 'if you want to get B, do A' and our definition of causality can be rephrased 'If when you do A, B follows, A is the cause of B.' In this sense we can logically infer a knowledge of causality from the successful production of D-scrapers and Moustierian points. The regular reproduction of the same standard form by the same process over many generations does indicate that a rule securing this regularity was inculcated and transmitted by society. The rule must then have been formulated in symbols and conceptualized. It must have included the prescription 'To get a flake like this, strike the core there with such and such strength at such and such an angle.'

The good archæologist who can himself detach such a flake from the core is in truth re-enacting in his own mind the thought of Moustierian man. He may not be able to express it as an equation and it is certain that he cannot formulate it precisely as the Moustierian would. The latter's rule would probably run something like this. 'To make a D-scraper, collect a flint nodule (1) at full moon, (2) after fasting all day, (3) address him politely with "words of power" (4) . . . strike him thus with a hammerstone, (5) smeared with the blood of a sacrificed mouse.' Technical and scientific progress has of course just been discovering that (1), (2), (3) and (5) are quite irrelevant to the success of the operation prescribed in (4). These acts were, we now know, futile accessories, expressive of ideological delusions. It is just these that have been erased from the archæological record. Errors expunged, knowledge stands out all the clearer to be re-known.

But though the error, the ideological delusions, the superstitions have been expunged, the acts they inspired may have left a profound mark on the archæological record; that would indeed be jejune if stripped of tombs and temples! We can not only apprehend their fossilized results as archæological data; we should also try to appreciate their real historical function that need have nothing to do with the subjective intentions of the actors. We can and must for instance appraise the practical science applied in laying-out and erecting a megalithic tomb, its economic role in the accumulation of a social surplus and in the distribution of wealth, its value in cementing as well as expressing social solidarity. Not one of these aspects of the ceremony is at all likely to have been present to the consciousness—a 'false consciousness'—of the architects and builders. Their 'motives', like their emotions, have been lost for ever, just because they were illusions. Does that matter?

Index

INDEX

INDEX